Fighting Inflation and Promoting Growth

A Statement
on National Policy
by the Research and Policy Committee
of the Committee
for Economic Development

August 1976

Library of Congress Cataloging in Publication Data

Committee for Economic Development.
  Fighting inflation and promoting growth.

   1. Inflation (Finance)--United States. 2. United
States--Economic policy--1971-   I. Title.
HG538.C799   1976   332.4'1'0973   76-25444 8/31/81
ISBN 0-87186-761-3   lib. bdg.
ISBN 0-87186-061-9   pbk.

First printing: August 1976
Paperbound: $2.50
Library binding: $4.00
Printed in the United States of America by Georgian Press, Inc.
Design: Harry Carter

COMMITTEE FOR ECONOMIC DEVELOPMENT
477 Madison Avenue, New York, N.Y. 10022

Contents

Responsibility for CED Statements on National Policy

The Committee for Economic Development is an independent research and educational organization of two hundred business executives and educators. CED is nonprofit, nonpartisan, and nonpolitical. Its purpose is to propose policies that will help to bring about steady economic growth at high employment and reasonably stable prices, increase productivity and living standards, provide greater and more equal opportunity for every citizen, and improve the quality of life for all. A more complete description of the objectives and organization of CED is to be found on page 96.

All CED policy recommendations must have the approval of the Research and Policy Committee, a group of sixty trustees whose names are listed on these pages. This Committee is directed under the bylaws to "initiate studies into the principles of business policy and of public policy which will foster the full contribution by industry and commerce to the attainment and maintenance" of the objectives stated above. The bylaws emphasize that "all research is to be thoroughly objective in character, and the approach in each instance is to be from the standpoint of the general welfare and not from that of any special political or economic group." The Committee is aided by a Research Advisory Board of leading social scientists and by a small permanent professional staff.

4

The Research and Policy Committee is not attempting to pass judgment on any pending specific legislative proposals; its purpose is to urge careful consideration of the objectives set forth in this statement and of the best means of accomplishing those objectives.

Each statement on national policy is preceded by discussions, meetings, and exchanges of memoranda, often stretching over many months. The research is undertaken by a subcommittee, assisted by advisors chosen for their competence in the field under study. The members and advisors of the subcommittee that prepared this statement are listed on page 6.

The full Research and Policy Committee participates in the drafting of findings and recommendations. Likewise, the trustees on the drafting subcommittee vote to approve or disapprove a policy statement, and they share with the Research and Policy Committee the privilege of submitting individual comments for publication, as noted on this and the following page and on the appropriate page of the text of the statement.

Except for the members of the Research and Policy Committee and the responsible subcommittee, the recommendations presented herein are not necessarily endorsed by other trustees or by the advisors, contributors, staff members, or others associated with CED.

6

Foreword

Purpose of This Statement

THE INTRACTABLE NATURE OF THE PROBLEM of maintaining growth in the economy with stable prices and high employment can be illustrated in many ways. One way is to observe that 25 of the total 109 policy statements issued by CED to date have been devoted to the problem. This latest effort was set in motion in May 1973, as the inflation rate soared. Later, as the subcommittee went into a series of monthly meetings, its task was compounded by a sharp recession and an increase in unemployment to the highest rate since World War II.

Our effort to grapple with the events that occurred during the period of preparation considerably deepens our understanding of modern-day inflation. Chapter 1 identifies the shocks that contributed to the violent upsurge of prices which continued through the recession as significant factors for special policy consideration. We then suggest measures supplementary to fiscal and monetary policies for preventing or moderating a recurrence of instability of prices and employment. We concluded that the nation needs a mixture of many different measures tailored to blunt the progression of inflationary effects of shocks, with the main burden of stabilization resting on fiscal policies and much less on monetary policy. We also point to the need for government machinery that can put the appropriate policies into action when they are needed. Wage and price guidelines and mandatory controls are rejected except in emergency wartime conditions.

The Committee reaffirms its recommendation of a national policy goal of high employment without inflation. Even though the policy instruments that must be used to stabilize the economy in this condition are in the hands of the federal government, it has not enunciated a concerted program to bring inflation to an end. This being so, we call upon the President to propose such a program with a timetable for achieving national goals for high employment and growth without inflation. We propose further that Congress consider and act upon this program in conjunction with its setting of overall budget totals.

The statement is more explicit about the content of such a program than it may seem to be at first reading. It should be based on the premise that "no single policy will solve the inflation problem." It should rely basically on appropriate fiscal policies aimed in these times at larger high-employment budget surpluses than we have previously advocated. If such fiscal policies are followed, there should be less emphasis on monetary policy. But these macroeconomic policies should be accompanied by a variety of measures, including those designed to strengthen competitive forces, to reduce the impact of shocks derived from shortages of farm products and raw materials, and to moderate cost pressures in sectors such as health care, construction, and collective bargaining settlements in the public sector. The program should also provide ways to overcome capacity bottlenecks in energy and basic commodities.

As the statement concludes, we are not confident that "even if our total program were adopted, it would successfully stem inflation and promote growth." But the measures advocated are worth trying, and they are within our capacity to implement. We in CED will, as we have in the past, continue to study these problems. If the answers proposed here do not bring success, we will assess our progress and seek better ones.

We are indebted to John R. Coleman, the subcommittee chairman, for his patience, perseverance, and wisdom in bringing this project to a successful conclusion; to Barry Bosworth, the project director, for his knowledge and insight in his many draft proposals; and to Frank W. Schiff, our chief economist, for his assistance as associate project director. For unusual effort extending over fourteen meetings, we commend the members of the subcommittee and its advisors. The list of subcommittee members appears on page 6.

Very special gratitude is due Alfred C. Neal, retiring president of CED, for his contribution to the scope and form of this statement and to his vital role during the past two decades in guiding the formulation of the many CED positions on which this report is based. We are indebted to the Lilly Endowment for a grant that made it possible to meet ad hoc research requirements.

Philip M. Klutznick, *Chairman*
Research and Policy Committee
until May 19

Franklin A. Lindsay, *Chairman*
Research and Policy Committee
beginning May 20

Chapter 1

Introduction: The Changing Nature of Inflation

INFLATION IS PROBABLY THE MOST COMPLEX and unyielding economic problem of this generation. This Committee is dedicated to the long-term growth of the U.S. economy with stable prices and to a healthy society in which there is useful work for all who want to work. These goals are incompatible with a continuing high rate of inflation. We are firmly committed to finding ways of restraining inflation and restoring the economy to conditions of sustainable growth at high employment.*

Why are we concerned about inflation? A high inflation rate disrupts the economy and divides the society. Increasing prices erode the real purchasing power of savings and of invested capital. An inflationary surge interferes with rational output and investment decisions, contributes to social and industrial strife, and diverts an undue share of the nation's productive energies into efforts to beat the inflation spiral. It distorts and undermines financial market processes.

Inflation is also highly inequitable. It redistributes incomes in a capricious fashion, usually hitting hard at the weakest in the society, especially the poor, the aged, and the ill. These inequities are multiplied when, as has recently been the case, inflation is accompanied by severe economic recession and high unemployment.

A steep and stubborn inflation such as the most recent one dampens confidence in the nation's institutions and in its future. The expectation that inflation will persist becomes a self-fulfilling prophecy.

*See memoranda by JERVIS J. BABB, by FLETCHER L. BYROM, by EDWARD R. KANE, by FRAZAR B. WILDE, and by THEODORE O. YNTEMA, pages 78 to 80.

Our concern has been heightened by the sharp rise of the inflation rate in 1973 and 1974 and the fears of a recurrence in future years. Some of the events of this period clearly were beyond this country's complete control. A sequence of major disturbances in world markets for energy, food, and raw materials combined to fuel the worst inflation of the post-war period. The problems were compounded by excessive instability of fiscal and monetary policies, devaluation of the dollar, and a system of wage and price controls that distorted the allocation process.*

Although the rate of inflation has recently declined as a result of more stable energy prices, increased agricultural production, and a severe recession, inflation continues to menace the economy. The inflation rate has receded substantially from its double-digit levels of 1974, but it still remains unacceptably high, particularly for a period in which the economy is operating far below its potential. In addition, the costs of checking inflation through recession are high in terms of lost jobs and lost incomes, increased crime, and greater welfare payments. The United States faces great difficulties in attempting to restore high employment and price stability to the economy in the near future. A positive program for eliminating inflation and restoring high employment remains a matter of great urgency for the nation.**

INFLATION'S COMPLEX CAUSES

The traditional view has been that inflation results almost entirely from too much demand relative to supply (too much money chasing too few goods) and that unemployment results from too little demand relative to supply. Accordingly, economic policy decisions throughout the postwar period have often been presented as a choice between price stability and high employment. Unfortunately, both inflation and unemployment have become more severe in recent years. As Figure 1 illustrates, the annual average rate of inflation during 1975 was 7 percent, with unemployment averaging 8.5 percent. In the late fifties and early sixties, the rate of inflation rarely moved above 2 percent, and unemployment averaged about 5 percent.

Today, continued failure to resolve the inflation problem at high employment levels threatens the existence of the free-market economy. But a solution cannot be found by resorting to extremes. A high inflation rate is an intolerable cost to pay in the pursuit of low unemployment, just as

*See memorandum by ROBERT R. NATHAN, page 81.
**See memorandum by JOHN D. HARPER, page 82.

Figure 1: Inflation and Unemployment Changes, 1950 to 1975

In recent years, both unemployment and inflation rates rose to their highest levels in postwar history.

a Unemployment rates refer to annual averages. Changes in consumer prices refer to December-to-December changes.

Source: *Economic Report of the President, 1976* (Washington, D.C.: U.S. Government Printing Office, 1976).

high unemployment is an intolerable cost to pay in the search for price stability.

It has become obvious that the causes of the recent simultaneous high inflation and high unemployment are more complex than a simple matching of aggregate demand and supply would suggest. In examining these causes, we have found it useful to view the inflation process in terms of two distinct stages. First, there is an initial set of shocks that distort the existing wage and price structure. Such shocks may stem from excessive overall demand, but they can also be produced by numerous other factors, including serious disruptions of supply, major exchange rate adjustments, or anticipation of wage and price controls. Second, there is an adjustment period during which the initial disturbance is transmitted and magnified throughout the economy as other wages and prices move upward. It is this second stage that has proved to be very difficult to control by traditional measures of fiscal and monetary restraint even after the original disturbance has diminished.*

The exceptional magnitude of the recent inflation and its persistence in the face of the highest unemployment rates since 1941 can be explained largely by two factors. They were the unusual magnitude and rapid succession of the shocks to which the economy has been subjected and the fact that these shocks have impinged on an economic system which has tended to become less flexible over the years. Neither of these factors alone can account for the unexpected nature of the recent inflation. Indeed, most of the structural rigidities that make it so difficult for the economy to adjust to shocks in a noninflationary fashion have been present or have been developing for a considerable period of time. It is the *combination* of the two factors that, in the main, has brought about the type of inflation with which we have recently been confronted.

The characteristics of this inflation provide clear evidence of the distortions that can result from sudden changes in domestic economic conditions. They also underline the extent to which the U.S. economy is affected by changes in the world economy and the difficulty this country has faced in responding to international developments. The American economy is closely linked to a world economy that it cannot fully control. It is deeply affected by international developments at a time when its domestic economic policies have become more unstable and when the U.S. government has involved itself more heavily in the question of how resources should be allocated. Actions designed to restore high domestic employment and economic growth and to provide a more equal distribution of income all tend to exert an upward pressure on prices. Moreover,

*See memoranda by E. SHERMAN ADAMS, and by JOHN D. HARPER, page 82.

there has been little recognition of the economic problems posed by rapid political, social, and technological changes and little awareness of the fact that a market economy responds to such changes only with a considerable lag. What we find most disturbing are the expectations that inflation will continue at high levels and the growing willingness to tolerate such a situation.

Fiscal and monetary policies have been the traditional weapons for combating inflation.* Fiscal policy deals with the impact on the level of economic activity of changes in government taxes and expenditures. Monetary policy is concerned with the impact on prices and output of changes in the money supply and in the cost and availability of credit. These policies have been the major force for long-term economic stability.

Over the past decade, fiscal and monetary policies have not always been properly harmonized, nor have they been applied in a timely fashion. They have not been used in a manner that recognizes the complex and rapidly changing economic events of the recent past or those that will certainly occur in the future.

But even if fiscal and monetary remedies had been applied effectively, the burgeoning and spread of inflation during the 1973–1975 period would probably not have been fully avoided. Undoubtedly, both analysis and policies that go beyond traditional fiscal and monetary measures are required to deal with the changing nature of inflation. The conventional wisdom about taxing, public spending, and the money supply is still both relevant and highly important, but it is no longer enough.*

In recent statements on inflation, this Committee dealt extensively with the need to view the inflation problem in a broader perspective and to rely on a wide range of approaches to cope with it, in addition to more rational and flexible use of the traditional weapons. The sharp rise of the inflation rate in recent years, together with the failure to apply fiscal and monetary policies in a manner that produces satisfactory results, makes this present reexamination of the problem urgent business.

Sources of Economic Instability

The 1973–1975 inflationary episode has offered the sharpest example of the role played by forces other than excess demand, forces that in the short term, at least, may be strong enough to override traditional economic stabilization policies. They include changes in the world economy, severe economic shocks, and structural changes in the domestic economic system.

*See memoranda by JOHN D. HARPER, page 83.

Changes in the World Economy. The world has changed so much that the United States now stands in a less dominant relationship to other countries. The period during which domestic considerations overshadowed the U.S. role in the world economy has come to an end. Hence, sharp world competition for resources and the increased interdependence of national economies give the problem of inflation an expanded international scope. In fact, such changes have already made it painfully clear that the economic policies of other countries, including those of the developing nations, have a heavy bearing on U.S. domestic life. What other countries do about inflation affects the United States at once, and what this country does echoes abroad.

At the same time, important changes in the world economy have created increased opportunities for a more independent national economic policy. Foreign exchange rates are more flexible than they were under the old system of fixed parities, and an individual country can, if it chooses, avoid the importation of inflation from abroad as a result of excessive world demand for its products. For a country with a large balance-of-payments surplus, an upward revaluation of that country's exchange rates tends to restrict exports and stimulate imports; devaluation tends to produce the opposite result. Flexible exchange rates also have minimized some of the structural upheavals brought about by monetary disturbances either at home or in other important countries and have reduced the problems of destabilizing speculation that existed under the former system of pegged rates, which could be adjusted only by official decisions.

But greater flexibility in foreign exchange rates and increased integration of world financial markets have also brought increased complications. Some of the apparent pressure for domestic restraint of inflation has been lost because the effects of an excessive rise in domestic prices on a country's international position can be offset in part by devaluation. Attempts of the monetary authorities to stimulate or restrain demand within the domestic economy by changing interest rates may be countered by the outflow or inflow of capital in search of the most attractive interest rate yields.

Severe Shocks. International developments were largely responsible for the special and severe shocks that triggered the most recent inflation. These took the form of serious disruptions of supply and prices of food, raw materials, and energy. The importance of the energy and food components of the rate of increase in the consumer price index is illustrated in Figure 2.

First, a severe worldwide crop failure led to a sharp expansion of U.S. agricultural exports at a time when reserve stocks had been reduced to low levels. The result was a 35 percent rise in the food component of the consumer price index during 1973–1974. Second, a worldwide shortage of raw materials, together with the U.S. devaluation, raised U.S. import prices at an annual rate of 26 percent between the first and third quarters of 1973. Third, the oil embargo in late 1973 helped trigger a fourfold increase in the world price of oil, which was followed by price hikes for other fuels and for a vast range of petroleum-based products. The steep increase in petroleum costs also represented a drastic "tax" on incomes in the United States and other oil-importing countries. Thus, although it raised costs and prices directly, it reduced aggregate demand in real terms and hence contributed to the recession. Fourth, these factors were exacerbated by a system of price controls in the United States that restricted the normal expansion of supply in some markets and created shortages that could be eliminated only by major price increases once controls were removed in 1974.

During this same period, two formal dollar devaluations and a loosely managed exchange rate system tended to cheapen U.S. exports in world markets and to raise import price levels sharply. Much (although probably not all) of the exchange rate adjustment had been long overdue, but the suddenness and magnitude of its impact intensified the short-run pressures on price levels. This sequence of shocks, beginning in 1972, led to a sharp acceleration of the inflation rate to double-digit levels by late 1973. Double-digit inflation continued until late 1974, running at an annual rate of some 14 percent. With the recession, the rate of increase in prices slowed; and by early 1976, consumer prices were rising at about 4.5 percent per year.

Except for devaluation of the dollar, these disturbances reflected changes in relative prices only. But in order for the overall price level to have remained unchanged after the increase in the prices of food, energy, and raw materials, other prices and wages would have had to decline by more than 3 percent. Within the structure of the U.S. economy, such a reduction of prices would have required extreme and probably intolerable measures of demand restraint.

But the problem generated by these shocks was not limited to the direct price effects. The decline in living standards resulting from price increases initiated demands for compensating income increases for wage and salary workers and for producers of other commodities and services whose prices had lagged. Average first-year settlements under larger

Figure 2: Inflation's Changing Mix (quarter-to-quarter change at an annual rate)

During 1973, sharp upward pressure on food prices contributed substantially to the overall rise in the consumer price index, as did both food and energy prices a year later. Moreover, the dramatic increase in prices in these two components created inflationary shocks that were transmitted to the nonfood and nonenergy sectors. In 1974, all components of the consumer price index contributed heavily to the overall rate of increase in consumer prices. The contribution to inflation from the food and energy sectors moderated considerably in 1975, but these components still contributed, both directly and indirectly, to the overall rate of inflation. Only in the first quarter of 1976 did food and energy prices show an actual decline, thus reducing the overall inflation rate to 4.5 percent. In other commodity and service sectors, inflation continued at a high rate.

union contracts doubled from 5.5 percent per year in the last quarter of 1973 to 11 percent per year in the third quarter of 1974. Within the private nonfarm economy, increases in hourly compensation accelerated from 6.7 percent during 1972 to 10.7 percent during 1974. Thus, the efforts of individuals and groups to pass on the costs of a lower living standard to others caused the inflation to spread rapidly throughout the economy.

Structural Changes*

In recent decades, the structure of the domestic economic system has changed considerably in ways that have increased its inflationary bias.**

■ The growing importance of labor unions and collective bargaining and the increased specialization of labor have sharply altered the nature of the wage-determination process.

■ The increased importance of fixed costs of invested capital and long lead times means that decisions to enter a new product market or to expand existing capacity must be based on long-term considerations rather than on purely cyclical market developments. In combination with the highly

*See memoranda by ROBERT R. NATHAN, and by HERMAN L. WEISS, pages 83 and 84.
**See memorandum by JOHN D. HARPER, page 84.

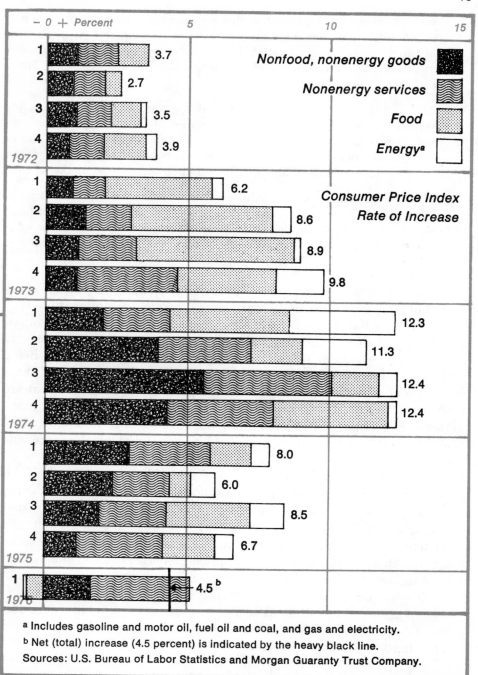

a Includes gasoline and motor oil, fuel oil and coal, and gas and electricity.
b Net (total) increase (4.5 percent) is indicated by the heavy black line.
Sources: U.S. Bureau of Labor Statistics and Morgan Guaranty Trust Company.

specialized nature of production that results from economies of scale and product differentiation, high fixed costs limit the short-run responsiveness of supply to increased demand. In particular, episodes of inflation have greatly reduced the recovery of real capital because depreciation is based on original cost.

- The growth of the public sector, expanded government regulation of the private sector, and the declining importance of the more price-competitive sectors such as agriculture mean that in an increasing proportion of the economy prices and wages are heavily influenced by factors other than the competitive demand and supply conditions of specific markets.*

- More comprehensive and sustaining income maintenance programs make it possible to cushion the impact of inflation and unemployment on large segments of the population. At the same time, overcompensation for inflation in the benefits provided in some of these programs has itself become inflationary.

Some of these factors are new; some have been developing for many years but have only recently become more obvious. In combination, they yield a system that can adjust to sharp changes in economic conditions only with a significant time lag and with considerable transition costs and conflicts. Yet, events of recent years suggest that the economy is being faced with larger and more abrupt requirements for change. Some of these structural changes are reversible, and the parts of the economy that are least responsive to market forces can be made more responsive. But many of these changes have been dictated by the advance of technology and by changing public views of what should be expected of the economic system.

This conclusion implies a great deal more about the 1973–1975 inflation than may be obvious. The severe shocks of that period were deeply disturbing to the changed structure of the U.S. economy. An economy that has such difficulty adjusting to rapid changes of the kind we have outlined can encounter the anomaly of simultaneous inflation and recession. Shocks can result in spreading the effects of price increases even in the face of falling aggregate demand and increasing unemployment because not enough offsetting price decreases occur. Thus, the system can become insulated against the traditional decline in the average level of prices during recessions. (The reasons for this change in behavior will be discussed more extensively later in this chapter.) However, inflation is clearly not wholly immune to recession; witness the sharp reduction in the pace of consumer price increases between late 1974 and early 1976.

*See memorandum by JOHN D. HARPER, page 85.

Lessons of the Past

It is not enough to understand the causes of the recent inflation; to fully comprehend its unusual dimensions, it must be contrasted with earlier inflation episodes. Because inflation has often been associated with an excessive level of aggregate demand, it is believed that more effective demand management is an important action that should be taken to prevent or moderate inflation. However, the historical record strongly suggests that this is not enough. The economy experiences persistently rising prices despite the existence of a level of demand that leaves a considerable proportion of resources unemployed. Particularly in recent years, demand restraint has contributed to plunging the economy into severe recessions without bringing the inflation of prices and wages to an end; most of the fall in demand was met by adjusting output and employment rather than by reducing prices or wages. Cuts in some prices and wages become prevalent only after a substantial period of demand restraint and in a context in which many other prices and wages are inflexible or rising.*

Four Inflation Episodes. Since 1950, the United States has had four major episodes of accelerating inflation. The role of excess demand has varied significantly among them.

1950–1951. Both prices and wages rose sharply in late 1950 in response to major increases in demand brought on by the outbreak of the Korean War. But the inflation was also fueled by expectations of future wartime shortages and speculative activity in the basic commodity markets. In the subsequent years, reduced fears of shortages led to a sharp reversal of the earlier commodity price increases, and wage and price controls succeeded in preventing a spread of the inflation into successive cycles of wage and price increases within other sectors. As a result, the inflation rate declined sharply despite extremely high levels of overall resource utilization; the unemployment rate averaged less than 3 percent in 1952–1953.

1956–1957. In 1956 and 1957, prices and wages again rose sharply despite less growth in aggregate demand than in supply. Although the strong rise in demand in 1955 was an important initiating factor, the inflation rate accelerated in 1956 and 1957 in the face of a slow growth of demand. Explanations of this inflation episode emphasized the imbalance of demand pressures among industries because wage and price increases in sectors of

*See memorandum by JOHN D. HARPER, page 85.

strong demand were not fully offset by wage and price declines in industries with sagging demand. The inflation was brought to a halt only by the outbreak of severe recession in late 1957.

1965–1971. The acceleration of price increases between 1965 and 1969 may have been primarily a reflection of an excessive level of aggregate demand as Vietnam War expenditures were imposed on a fully employed economy without concurrent increases in taxes or reductions in other government outlays. A timely and coordinated policy of fiscal and monetary restraint should have been an important part of the corrective actions.

But the continuation of the inflation in 1970 and 1971, after the shift of policy to extreme demand restraint, is difficult to relate to any concurrent situation of excess demand. Nor is it consistent with earlier evidence on the lag between a slowing of economic activity and deceleration of price inflation. Instead, it seems to have been maintained by the efforts of groups that had fallen behind in the previous inflation to restore their relative income positions. General expectations of continuing price inflation also may have made the income increases easier to achieve despite conditions of adequate or excess supply that existed in most markets. In addition, the inflation was sustained by extreme increases of prices and wages within specific industries such as construction, medical care, and public services.

1973–1975. * In 1972, the economy was recovering from recession, and the inflation of both wages and prices was moderating under the influence of improved productivity growth and wage and price controls; domestic nonfarm prices rose at an annual rate of less than 3 percent in late 1972. However, monetary and fiscal policies were overly expansionary in late 1972 and contributed to an excessive growth in aggregate demand in early 1973. The economy was then disrupted by the series of severe shocks described earlier. These shocks, together with structural changes in the economy, upset the traditional adjustment process and produced a combined inflation and recession. Although a similar condition of stagflation had emerged in 1956–1957 and 1970–1971, the magnitude of increases in inflation and unemployment rates during the 1973–1975 period was unprecedented in postwar history.

*See memorandum by HERMAN L. WEISS, page 85.

The record of the past does not exhaust the list of potentia[l]
of inflation; unpredictable kinds of inflationary disturbances are lik[e]
occur in the future. What these four episodes do make clear is that [no]
single approach to inflation is appropriate for all times. Policies designed
to eliminate excess demand pressures are not appropriate to counter the
inflation effect of crop failures, specific industry problems, distortions
of the relative wage structure, and other sources of supply disruption.
Rather, they suggest the need for a variety of corrective measures that can
be applied in a discriminating fashion. In addition, it appears that the
length of time required to restore price stability after an initiating shock
has steadily lengthened in successive postwar cycles and that the rate of
unemployment consistent with a return to price stability is becoming
intolerably high.

PROBLEMS OF ADJUSTMENT*

As noted earlier, the inflation process can be viewed in terms of two
stages: an initial set of shocks and an adjustment period during which
the initial disturbance is transmitted throughout the economy. The economy does not adapt quickly to such a disturbance. The adjustment of
output and resource use is made difficult by lags in changing stabilization
policy, by the resistance of some wages and prices to downward pressures, and by the inherent short-run rigidity of a highly specialized
industrial economy.

The free-market system has proved highly adaptable to economic
change over the long term, and it should not be abandoned in a difficult
period of adjustment. With adequate time, capacity can be increased,
contracts can be renegotiated, and substitute products and services can
be found. But in a system where the generation of new productive capacity takes many years, where individual products are highly specialized
in both their production and their application, and where large amounts
of special skills are required of labor, sudden and extreme changes in
the demand for individual products cannot be quickly met. Thus, in
industries operating near capacity levels of output, supply is often not
highly responsive to price increases in the short run because resources
cannot be quickly moved. Nor in periods of slack is new capacity always
added with sufficient lead time to meet the next cycle in expansion of
demand. These adjustment problems are intensified by institutional ar-

*See memorandum by HERMAN L. WEISS, page 86.

...ind labor markets that result in a resistance
...es and by difficulties in distinguishing be-
...rm imbalances.

...age Adjustments

...ons has been an important means of improv-
...provides the individual worker with some
...: in a large and complex industrial society.
...altered the process of wage determination.
The acceptance or rejection of a specific wage offer has become a group
rather than an individual decision; and in combination with the right
to strike and picketing, this group decision represents a significant depar-
ture from a simple view of competitive markets. For many union members, the fear of unemployment as a result of excessive wage increases
has been reduced by job seniority provisions that concentrate the risks
and costs of unemployment upon the last hired. Competitive pressures
may prevent a significant long-run change in relative wages between
union and nonunion industries, but the process of overall wage negotiation becomes much more of a ratchet process as different groups attempt
to improve or restore their relative income positions regardless of underlying market changes in the demand for their services. Although unions
represent a minority of the work force, they exert a strong influence on
wages of associated workers. In addition, many other professional organizations maintain a strong group control over incomes and the supply
of labor even though they are not formally referred to as unions.

Moreover, the process of realigning wage rates is spread over a
long period because of the highly diverse nature of U.S. labor markets
and of the collective bargaining process. As a result, the disparities that
develop in the wage structure stretch the period of adjustment far
beyond the initial disturbance.

Price Adjustments

A similar evolution has occurred in many product markets. In certain
cases, high levels of technological specialization together with economies
of scale have tended to require only a few producers of a specific product
at any given time. Such product specialization contributes to lower prices
over the long term through more efficient production. Competitive forces
normally prevent this situation from giving rise to high profits on a long-

run basis because new firms can eventually enter the market if rates of return stay high. But the decision to expand supply through the entry of new firms or additions to the capacity of existing firms must be based on long-term considerations of future cost-price relationships. Thus, this trend has reduced the short-run response of supply to increased demand. The low price sensitivity of demand faced by firms in such specialized industries limits incentives to cut prices as a means of maintaining revenue during recessions.

Price reductions in recessions have also been moderated by the operation of restrictive trade laws, by the sensitivity of Western countries to demands for quota protection in certain industries where both management and labor are politically active, by unnecessarily rigid regulatory practices, and by limited price competition in those markets where the presence of few firms cannot be explained by economies of scale in production and distribution.*

Effects of Long-Term Contracts

The process of inflation is also affected by long-term contracts in labor, capital, and product markets. It is more difficult to achieve changes in price and wage trends in response to changing market conditions when prices and wages are individually set at separate intervals rather than being continuously reviewed and revised. Long-term contracts are an essential characteristic of an advanced capital-intensive economy, but the distortions and inequities that can result when these contracts fail to anticipate the actual inflation rate are likely to result in continued inflationary changes in future years when contracts are renegotiated. The same inflationary effect is also possible when wage increases are written into second, third, or later years of a contract and these increases turn out to be much in excess of the cost-of-living changes that the increases contemplated. A natural consequence of this problem is a growing use of escalator provisions in long-term contracts, but those provisions in themselves feed the next round of inflation unless the higher wages, rates, and prices are offset by higher productivity.

Government Influences

Major changes in the relationship between the government and the private sector have also contributed to the problems of adjustment. Today, the government sector accounts for nearly one-fifth of nonagricultural

*See memoranda by JOHN R. COLEMAN, by JOHN D. HARPER, and by R. HEATH LARRY, page 86.

employment, compared with about one-eighth after World War II. This growth has been combined with a major change in the process of wage determination. In government, unionized bargaining coexists with a much lower risk of unemployment than in the private sector and without the countervailing pressures of the competitive market. In such bargaining, political considerations may outweigh the economic ones. The tax structure has not been adapted to take account of its effects on investment incentives and the problems of maintaining investment during inflationary periods. Government regulations have frequently ignored the adjustment problem and have unnecessarily constrained the ability of the regulated sectors to respond to changed competitive conditions. In the design of new government programs, little or no attention has been paid to the lags involved in shifting resources to meet new needs. Some of these programs and regulatory aims are highly desirable, but there may be alternative means of achieving the same ends. In the past, the evaluation of these alternatives has reflected too little concern with their inflationary impact.

Struggle to Maintain Living Standards

There may be no more powerful and important struggles in the United States over the next decade than the fights to maintain or improve both one's real buying power and one's relative position on the income ladder. Inflation is a cause and an effect of that struggle. Indeed, to the extent that inflation is a manifestation of more general social problems, it cannot be viewed strictly as an economic phenomenon. In the struggle to maintain living standards, some groups are granted larger money income increases on the basis of equity considerations or because of threats to disrupt critical services, not because of market conditions or because there is a shortage of the services that they supply. Increases are promised to some without the explicit or even tacit agreement of others to accept less. The process resembles a rerunning of the *Alice in Wonderland* caucus race, in which "everyone has won, and all shall have prizes." Thus, the direct conflict that would otherwise result is postponed. This process of promising more to everyone is bound to result in inflation because prices are raised to reflect higher costs in one sector without offsetting price reductions in others. Unless everyone receives the same percentage escalation, the real income of some will fall behind. But the process by which money incomes are scaled back in real terms is an impersonal one. Everyone believes that his own income increase is deserved and that inflation results from outside forces or from the unjustified demands of others.

The means of resolving conflicting demands on the distribution of income may be affordable as long as the demands remain within bounds. But as the participants anticipate the future inflation, they escalate their own demands, and the costs become heavier. The costs are further compounded when special-interest groups protect themselves from the restraint of the market by forming larger power blocs or by obtaining political intervention on their behalf. Unless these escalating demands are checked or unless an alternative means of resolving such conflicting demands can be found, a system based on competition could become a system based on coercion.

The process of adjusting relative incomes through continually escalating demands is a highly ineffective means of dealing with the underlying problems. Not all members of society can protect themselves through such a process, particularly the least organized. Moreover, the process may get out of control (as it has in other countries) and lead to still greater inequities. The difficulties and uncertainties involved in a reallocation of resources through distortions of income shares may have particularly disruptive effects on the efficient operation and continuation of a free-market system.

The struggle to maintain living standards is illustrated by recent events. American labor and capital became less scarce relative to food, fuel, and foreign production in 1973 and 1974 and hence less valuable. However, there was too little acceptance of the fact that, following food and raw materials shortages, energy price increases, devaluation, and increased social security taxes, the average standard of living had to decline for all Americans until productivity increases could catch up with the shocks of inflation. Instead, various groups have preferred to battle over who will do the adjusting, with each group maintaining that its efforts are aimed only at maintaining its previous position. The result has been an upward spiral of wages, prices, and social security benefits, a severe tightening of stabilization policy in response to inflation fears, recession, and a far larger loss of real incomes than was ever required by the initial disturbance.

The important conclusion is not that the existing income distribution is the correct one or that it cannot be changed; rather, attempts to improve individual standards of living through the process of escalating demands in the labor market are likely to be highly inflationary, even more inequitable than other methods, and in the end, self-defeating. It is preferable by far to seek any changes that might be warranted in the overall distribution of income through a procedure that represents all the views of society and that interferes least with free-market processes needed for efficient resource allocation. Such mechanisms already exist within the political process of determining tax rates and transfer payments.*

FISCAL AND MONETARY POLICIES: WHAT WENT WRONG?

Although a wide range of anti-inflation weapons may be useful, fiscal and monetary policies have been and should continue to be the fundamental instruments for stabilizing the economy. Fiscal and monetary policies are broad and general in character, designed at their best to keep the price structure stable and employment high without intervening in particular markets, although some markets are usually affected more than others. Fiscal and monetary policies require intelligent, skillful, and responsible management. They should be used to prevent inflation, not just to dampen it once it has begun.

Many of the difficulties encountered in the use of fiscal and monetary policies have stemmed from faulty management. The historical record shows that fiscal and monetary policies have suffered from mistakes of application, lack of coordination, time lags and delays, and an absence of reliable information. Above all, they must be applied with the political will to make them work. Unfortunately, that will is often conspicuously absent when proper fiscal policy would call for a tax increase to restrain an overheated economy. As a matter of practical politics, monetary policy is at times the only tool available.

Both fiscal and monetary policies can be either *built-in* or *discretionary*. Built-in responses perform their stabilizing function automatically by dampening expansions or contractions of economic activity. Discretionary policies can have either a stabilizing or a destabilizing effect and require specific decisions to activate them.

Built-in Stabilizers

The role of automatic stabilizers is most evident in the area of fiscal policy, where much of the tax system and some major expenditure programs are geared to the level of economic activity. In an economic expan-

*See memorandum by R. HEATH LARRY, page 87.

sion, tax revenues rise along with incomes (indeed, more rapidly than incomes because of the progressiveness of the income tax), and transfer payments (e.g., unemployment insurance) decline. This automatically shifts the government budget toward restraint during an expansion; at unchanged tax rates, government income increases, and its expenditures tend to decline.

However, the effects of built-in stabilizers are not always appropriate. These automatic devices can dampen the cycles of aggregate demand, but they sometimes make it more difficult to achieve desirable changes in the level of aggregate demand because they make no distinctions among the various causes of destabilization. The appropriate policy action may vary with the nature of the particular inflationary disturbances. For example, the response of fiscal and monetary policies should not be the same for a temporary rise in food prices following major crop failures as it is for a general rise of wages and prices resulting from excessive demand throughout the economy.

Despite these difficulties, the postwar record indicates that built-in stabilizers have been an important element in preventing the very large fluctuations in demand that plagued the economy in earlier periods.

Discretionary Policy

The historical record of discretionary policy (focusing on changes in tax rates and government expenditures) has not been very good. Too frequently, the timing of adjustments in policy has strengthened rather than dampened the cyclical fluctuations in economic activity. In part, these mistakes are due to unreliable information. Certain methods and data used for predicting future trends in the economy have proved faulty or inadequate. But these mistakes have sometimes been due to political hesitancy (or complete failure) to make policy adjustments when reliable data were at hand and the need for such adjustments was reasonably clear. Nonetheless, it is understandable that the politician who must soon stand before the electorate will exercise extreme caution in approving a tax increase based on necessarily uncertain economic forecasts of overheated growth.

Equally important, policies have fluctuated, not because of anticipated changes in economic conditions, but because of vacillation with respect to the goals of the policies themselves or a tendency to move to the extremes of restraint or expansion. Too often, the goal has been viewed simplistically: either to dampen inflation or to curb unemployment.

CED'S STABILIZING BUDGET POLICY

Over the past thirty years, CED's Research and Policy Committee has developed and enunciated through its policy statements a set of broad principles designed to guide the formulation of fiscal and monetary policies appropriate for economic stability as well as for efficient resource allocation and steady economic growth. The main principles can be summarized as follows:

The impact of the budget should vary with the condition of the economy as a whole, being more expansive when the economy is depressed and more restrictive when the economy is booming or inflationary.

The overall impact that the budget exerts upon the economy should not, when combined with appropriate monetary and other policies, be so restrictive that it makes attainment of high employment ordinarily unlikely or so expansive that it leads to persistent inflation.

Rarely have these two interrelated goals been balanced and treated with equal importance. Also, because many changes in economic policies exert an impact on the economy only after a considerable lag, there will always be a need to deal with the uncertainties of future economic conditions. But these uncertainties can be reduced by clarifying the stabilization policy objectives at the outset and shortening the lag required to make changes in them.

In addition, discretionary monetary and fiscal policies have often been poorly coordinated and internally inconsistent. Policies designed to deal with one set of circumstances may have served only to exacerbate another. Given the way our institutions have operated, fiscal policy has usually responded to conditions of recession, and monetary policy has been forced to undertake most of the restraint during periods of excessive demand expansion. The result has been several recent periods during which an ailing economy has been given the treatment of tight money and

To achieve these objectives, the federal government should normally set its expenditure programs and tax rates at levels that would yield a moderate budget surplus on a national income and product account basis under conditions of high employment and price stability.

The high-employment budget position should permit an adequate flow of funds to the private credit markets and to the markets for state and local securities, should not call for excessive tightness of monetary policy, and should help to promote sound economic growth.

Variations in tax yields, which rise and fall proportionately more than national income, and changes in government expenditures for unemployment assistance and other programs when unemployment changes, tend to cushion variations in total personal income and thereby lessen fluctuations in demand.

If demand conditions deviate significantly from those on which the stabilizing budget is based, flexible adjustments in a stabilizing direction should be made in income tax rates.

larger government deficits simultaneously. As implemented, monetary policy normally has had a greater effect on capital formation, and fiscal policy has had a stronger impact on consumption. Therefore, this trend in the mix of stabilization policies has intensified the long-run inflation problem by inhibiting the growth of productive capacity.

A consideration of the poor historical record for discretionary policy naturally leads to consideration of two possible approaches to reform: greater reliance upon fixed rules and automatic stabilizers or an effort to improve the conduct of discretionary policy. The magnitude of the shocks that the economy has recently experienced and the special problems that those shocks introduced are vivid examples of the difficulties of relying on fixed rules for either fiscal or monetary policy. The private economy is subject to significant disruptive shocks, and the period of adjustment to them is usually long. Greater reliance upon fixed rules might increase rather than reduce the instability of demand. Thus, there is need and potential for a positive stabilizing contribution by discretionary policies.

Although discretionary policies have not consistently played the stabilizing role assigned to them, we still believe that they can be made to work more promptly and effectively. If this is to be the case, however, the roles of monetary and fiscal policies in stabilizing the economy must be reconsidered. Finally, the authority and competence of government to manage fiscal and monetary policies effectively requires clear goals and constructive and determined political leadership.

POLICIES FOR FIGHTING INFLATION

Our analysis of the nature of the recent inflation suggests two broad areas in which new public policies may be effective. These policy approaches (which are discussed in detail in Chapters 2 and 3) involve *strengthening resistance to economic shocks* and to other disruptions of normal market processes and *curbing the spread of inflation* once the shocks have occurred.

Strengthening Resistance to Economic Shocks

The economy's resistance to disturbances that initiate an inflation may be strengthened in a number of ways. Efforts can be made to prevent inflationary pressures from developing through a more timely and less erratic use of fiscal and monetary policies. The economy might be better shielded from international disturbances through improved international consultation and cooperation and through international agreements on trade and monetary matters. A reserve stocks policy may help to overcome food shortages and to stabilize food prices. Actions can be taken to restructure certain problem industries such as construction and medical services and to improve collective bargaining in the public sector. The government can take steps to reduce the inflationary impact of its own operations, particularly its regulatory practices. Finally, incentives can be provided to expand productive capacity where it is most needed.

Curbing the Spread of Inflation

The difficulties of dampening an ongoing inflation reinforce the importance of focusing efforts on avoiding the initiating factors. Still, as

recent experience indicates, inflation can persist even after n[...]
initiating factors have been reversed. Therefore, measures are n[...]
curb the spread of inflation once the initial shocks have activated a[...]
and price spiral and inflation and recession have become embedde[...]
the economy. We examine two categories of alternatives for curbing th[...]
spread of inflation: efforts to strengthen competition so that market forces
can better succeed in dampening an inflation with a modest restraint of
aggregate demand and varying degrees of government participation in
holding down inflationary wage and price increases.

We believe that no single policy will solve the problem of inflation.
In the following chapters, we outline a program on many different fronts
for resolving the dilemma of inflation with recession.

any of the
eeded to
wage
d in

engthening Resistance
to Economic Shocks

THE PROBLEM OF HOW TO BOLSTER the economy's resistance to shocks is, in many ways, less intractable than the issue of how to end an inflation in which the distortions and inequities have already become severe. In particular, we believe that progress can be made in improving fiscal and monetary stabilization policies, in adjusting to changing relationships in the international economy, in dealing with structural changes in certain problem industries, in improving government regulatory procedures, and in creating incentives for a more timely adjustment of capacity in basic industries that have high overhead costs.

STRENGTHENING FISCAL POLICY

In measuring the effects of fiscal policy, a distinction should be made between the induced changes in the budget balance that result from operation of the built-in tax and expenditure stabilizers and those changes that result from discretionary adjustments in tax rates and expenditure programs. Thirty years ago, this Committee developed the stabilizing budget policy, which emphasized the distinction between the effect of the budget on the economy and the effect of the economy on the budget.

According to this policy, expenditure programs and tax rates should be set to yield a slight surplus at high employment and stable prices. It made clear that actual budget deficits which resulted from the operation of automatic stabilizers at a time of economic weakness were desirable as a means of stabilizing the economy. But by the same token, actual budget surpluses would be required when excessive levels of demand exerted upward pressure on prices and wages. In subsequent statements, the Committee concluded that additional discretionary policies may be required to bring about the desired stabilization objectives.

We recommend that the administration and the House and Senate Budget committees adhere to a stabilizing budget policy with federal tax rates and expenditures normally set to yield a small surplus at an agreed high level of employment and price stability. For the future, we recommend study of the desirability of modifying this rule so that the government can aim for a sizable surplus at high employment to help meet expanded needs for capital. In a companion study on capital needs, this Committee is giving detailed consideration to the issues involved in setting such guidelines.

We continue to believe that the basic objective with respect to prices should be the attainment of price stability, not merely some reduction in the rate of inflation. We identify absence of price inflation with stability in the consumer price index after allowing for the inability of this index fully to reflect quality changes in the production of goods and services. We recognize, moreover, that interim goals for the reduction of inflation under current government programs cannot realistically call for the complete elimination of inflationary tendencies within a very short period of time.

Similarly, in the case of employment, the basic goal should not be merely to reduce the level of overall unemployment to a given percentage of the labor force; rather, it should be to achieve a situation in which the number of job openings essentially matches the number of those seeking jobs at reasonable wages. Specific targets based on this measure should reflect changes in the structure of the labor market, efforts to improve job training, and strengthened work incentives. During the next few years, we believe that an unemployment rate near 5 percent is both an achievable temporary goal and the highest continuing rate that we should tolerate for any significant period of time.

Much of the problem in conducting economic policy has resulted from the inability to use discretionary fiscal policy in a timely fashion. In the past, such changes have been the result of long decision lags by

FULL-EMPLOYMENT BUDGET

Full-employment receipts is an analytic concept based on the amount of income that would be generated if the economy were continually operating at full capacity (conventionally defined as a 4.0 percent unemployment rate for the civilian labor force). Similarly, *full-employment outlays* include only that portion of the outlays for benefits under the regular unemployment insurance program that would be paid if the economy were continuously operating at full capacity. They thus eliminate the fluctuations in actual outlays for these benefits resulting from year-to-year changes in the unemployment rate. The differences between these adjusted receipts and outlay estimates are called *full-employment budget margins*. Changes in these margins from one year to the next provide a rough measure of the impact of discretionary fiscal policy (i.e., excluding automatic stabilizers) on the economy.

FULL-EMPLOYMENT RECEIPTS AND OUTLAYS, FISCAL YEARS 1972 TO 1978 (billions of dollars)

	1972	1973	1974	1975	1976	1977	1978
Full-employment receipts	223.5	244	282	323	347	389	445
Full-employment outlays	228.9	245	267	317	363	386	422
Full-employment budget margin	−5.4	−1	6	15	−16	3	23

both the administration and Congress. The 1964 tax reduction was passed thirteen months after the original request. The 1968 tax increase was enacted more than two years after the need for it was widely recognized. In recent years, the time required to legislate a tax reduction has decreased, but there is little evidence that similar speed could be anticipated if a tax increase should become necessary. In addition, most of the year-to-year changes in the *high-employment budget* have been the result of uncoordinated changes in individual expenditure programs without a

Although the full-employment concept is traditionally defined in terms of a hypothetical 4.0 percent unemployment rate, any other rate would serve essentially the same analytic purpose, provided it remained fixed from year to year.

NOTE: This material is adapted from the budget of the U.S. government published in January 1976. (Data for 1972 to 1975, supplied by the Office of Management and Budget, have been added.) It is based on the unified-budget concept, and estimated or projected data from 1976 on are subject to revision in the light of more recent developments. According to the January 1976 *Economic Report of the President,* full- (or high-) employment budget data calculated on a national income accounts basis, which are more useful for measuring fiscal effects than unified-budget data, showed the following pattern for changes in budget margins for calendar years 1972 to 1975:

1972	*1973*	*1974*	*1975*
−8.4	7.5	25.4	−7.5

Preliminary estimates also indicate that implementation of the first con-current resolution on the budget passed by Congress in May 1976 would imply a shift in the high-employment budget on a national income accounts basis from a declining deficit in calendar year 1976 to a modest surplus in 1977.

means of balancing the total expenditures against available revenues.

Recently, important improvements have occurred in institutional processes. The new legislative procedures mandated by the Congressional Budget and Impoundment Control Act of 1974 and initiated during 1975 call for a more coordinated and comprehensive annual budget process that includes improved long-term planning. For the first time in its history, Congress is operating under a procedure that requires it to consider total federal expenditures and revenues together and to consider their effect on the economy.[1] But even before the enactment of the new budget legislation, the President's annual budget document had started to include a five-year projection of the budget balance based on existing expenditure programs and current tax rates. The new congressional budget process now also requires regular evaluations of the five-year budget outlook by the Congressional Budget Office. These innovations allow a more rational evaluation of the long-term effects of expenditure and revenue programs on overall resource allocation.

We commend the steps already taken by Congress to reform the congressional budget process and urge it to continue the momentum by fully implementing the provisions of the new budget legislation and by adhering strictly to the timetable of the new act.

Although the recent reforms should contribute significantly to a more rational budget-setting process, more must be done to improve the short-run flexibility of fiscal policy in a way that will minimize disruptive influences on long-run budget objectives.

The variation of the budget balance for stabilization purposes should focus on temporary broad adjustments in taxes and selected temporary expenditure programs such as extension of unemployment insurance for a reasonable period and countercyclical public service employment. The expenditure programs chosen should generally contain built-in mechanisms to assure that they will be automatically phased out as high employment is approached.

Expenditure programs that have very long lead times between approval and actual expenditure should not be relied upon for short-run stabilization needs. For example, only 7 percent of the funds for the accelerated public works program passed in September 1962 were spent during that fiscal year; over 50 percent of the funds were unspent after two years; and the program continued to generate outlays for another seven years. Similar lags tend to occur in defense spending and categorical grants to state and local governments. In responding to short-run economic conditions, emphasis should be placed on temporary actions that will take effect quickly and that will involve the least commitment in future budgets.

---

[1] For a fuller discussion of the implications of the new budget process, see the December 1975 statement by CED's Program Committee, *The New Congressional Budget Process and the Economy.*

These considerations strongly suggest an emphasis on broad and simple income tax changes when special stabilizing actions are required. Such adjustments can be scheduled over time, and their effects are spread broadly over the economy. In this regard, we feel that the appropriate fiscal policy has been hindered by an unwillingness to accept changes in tax rates as a regular part of the budgetary process, especially when it is necessary to *raise* taxes in order to restrain the economy. Each time a tax adjustment becomes necessary, the larger issue of tax reform is raised. As taxpayers, we may be in favor of reform, but tax reform is a continuing and controversial issue, largely unrelated to the question of stabilization policy. The consideration of complex issues of equity and economic incentives require time. Reform seldom results when decisions are made under the pressure of deadlines demanded by economic stabilization. **Decisions regarding short-term fiscal stabilization policy—that is, regarding the net fiscal stimulus or restraint that the budget as a whole should exert at any one time—should be clearly distinguished from decisions regarding longer-term issues of tax reform.** Even from the viewpoint of short-term stabilization, however, there can at times be justification for structuring tax changes in ways that help to moderate upward wage and other cost pressures. An example is the personal income tax reduction of 1975, which was designed to provide special tax relief to income groups that had been most seriously affected by inflation and unemployment.

This Committee suggested in earlier statements that the President should be empowered to raise or lower income taxes within specified limits subject to congressional veto as a means of ensuring prompt adjustments in fiscal policy. We continue to believe that adoption of such a procedure would be highly desirable. However, to some observers, this power was seen as an infringement of the congressional power to determine taxes. We are not overly concerned with the means by which such flexibility might be achieved, so long as some effective procedure is instituted. The past decade has clearly indicated that lags in responding to inflationary pressures can be costly once expectations adapt to a continuing rise of the price level and distortions and inequities become embedded in the structure of prices and wages.

Hence, we believe that an alternative approach should also be considered that would give Congress a substantially larger role in initiating discretionary tax changes than the one envisioned in our earlier proposal. **We recommend that if Congress does not empower the President to raise or lower taxes within specified limits, it should as an alternative periodically agree on the form for any future tax adjustment for stabilization** purposes. If requested by the executive branch or upon a finding by its own budget committees that the need exists, Congress should agree to treat legislation requesting a stabilizing change in income taxes as a privileged bill and bring it to a full vote within thirty days. This would ensure a prompt decision.

The timely use of discretionary fiscal policy clearly offers the opportunity to improve the performance of the economy by avoiding inflationary excesses on the one hand and the costs of excessive unemployment on the other. A recognition of this potential has led this Committee to support a broader role for such measures. However, with few exceptions, the Committee has not been impressed with the ability of the executive branch and of Congress to coordinate their actions in order to fulfill this potential, especially when the proper economic course is a tax increase. Automatic stabilizers or rules applied in an overly mechanistic fashion are insufficient to deal fully with the wide range of stresses to which the economy is subject. Unless the institutions of discretionary fiscal policy can be strengthened and made more effective, there will be an increased reliance placed upon monetary policy, and we believe that this would be an undesirable outcome.

ADJUSTING MONETARY POLICY

During the last decade, the role of monetary policy in economic stabilization has expanded significantly. However, this development has been of questionable value. The aggressive use of monetary policy has not had the broad and evenhanded impact on the economy that some of its proponents anticipated. Instead, its short-term effects have been heavily concentrated in the housing industry because of the structure and regulation of the mortgage finance and home building industries. The disruption of home building has resulted in serious cyclical strains on the industry and its suppliers. This instability has been the source of part of the large cost increases. The high variability of housing production has inhibited the introduction of more efficient capital-intensive production techniques and generated supply shortages during expansions. In addition, the effect of monetary restraint on mortgage lending has posed serious equity issues because of the type of credit rationing that has resulted, and it has significantly raised the risks and thus the costs of such lending.

Automatic credit rationing has also placed a heavy burden of adjustment on municipal borrowing and on borrowers with less than the highest credit ratings, usually the smaller firms. We believe that a less concentrated impact of monetary policy would be highly desirable.

Monetary policy affects other components of aggregate demand, but the lags in these effects may extend beyond the ability to forecast future economic conditions. As a result, monetary policy has at times accentuated rather than dampened variations in the strength of aggregate demand. Furthermore, to the extent that monetary policy impinges more heavily upon growth sectors and investment decisions, it can intensify future inflation problems. A short episode of monetary restraint can reduce current investment demand without seriously affecting future capacity. The problem has been that monetary restraint has not been a transitory phenomenon. Instead, there has been a persistent rise in the degree of monetary restraint (interrupted by brief swings toward excessive ease) that has resulted from a combination of inflation and more restrictive monetary policies. In the long run, the higher interest rates can only be viewed as an increased cost of capital formation that must be reflected in higher prices.

The problems associated with discretionary monetary policy may become more severe in future years as a result of rapid development of international capital markets. Efforts to restrain the domestic economy by slower growth of the money supply and a rise in interest rates can be offset by inflows of capital from foreign countries in response to those interest rates. In principle, these changes in capital flows should lead to compensatory changes in the value of the dollar in a world of flexible exchange rates. As a result, monetary restraint would be reflected in a rise of imports and reduced export demand. This type of revaluation of the exchange rate makes an effective contribution to the easing of domestic inflation through lower import prices, but it raises prices for the countries whose currencies are effectively devalued and invites counteradjustments of their economic policies. Thus, capital mobility may at times limit the independence of monetary policy even with flexible exchange rates.

Some of these problems can be reduced if monetary control is not made the cutting edge of stabilization policy. At least in the short run, stabilization policy frequently involves difficult choices between the goals of price stability and high employment. Despite the institutional problems, we believe that the President and Congress, as elected representatives of the people, have the primary responsibility for making basic stabilization policy decisions through the formulation of tax and expenditure policies.

Failures in fiscal policy have too often led to a call on monetary policy to perform a role that it cannot fulfill. Monetary policy should not be expected to substitute for a responsible fiscal policy; discretionary fiscal policy must be made viable for periods of abrupt economic change.

We recommend a change in the policy mix toward greater reliance on fiscal policy for stabilization purposes. To the extent that fiscal policy is conducted in the responsible and flexible manner we have recommended, monetary policy should be normally responsive to it. Under such circumstances, monetary policy should be neither highly expansionary nor highly restrictive. Except in those periods when the greater short-run responsiveness of monetary policy to abrupt changes in economic activity requires a more active temporary role, the focus of monetary policy should be on maintaining an efficient capital market for the transfer of funds between saving and investment. But we believe that the larger adjustments for stabilization should be accomplished through the broader tools of fiscal policy.*

VARIATIONS IN THE ROLE OF STABILIZATION POLICY

Not all episodes of inflation have identical causes or cures.** In the course of this study, we have identified three distinctly different major causes of inflation:

■ *The classical case of an excess of aggregate demand.* This is characterized by capacity or labor shortages across a broad spectrum of industries.

■ *A rise in the aggregate price level that results from a sharp shift of demand or supply in a few industries.* The downward rigidity of other prices leads to a situation in which relative price changes usually produce a rise of the average price level.

■ *Rising prices and labor costs in the absence of any excess demand pressures.* This is due largely to institutional factors such as strong power blocs that are able to achieve price and wage increases despite the absence of high demand for their products or services or structural changes initiated by government programs or regulations that raise costs.

Certainly, in the case of general excess demand, it is clear that demand restraint must be the most important of any corrective actions. The primary need is for a faster policy response that will not concentrate the burden of restraint on just a few sectors. A quick response is required in order to minimize the distortions of relative wages and prices that become so evident once an inflation is well under way. Once this happens, institutional factors tend to take on greater importance. Wages and prices are much easier to raise than to lower; workers become more concerned with restoring previous wage differentials; and firms view their own price increases as being dictated by cost increases beyond their control. In addition, price stability is more difficult to restore once expectations of continuing inflation become solidly established.

However, extreme forms of demand restraint may make little or no contribution under other inflation conditions. For example, it may be wiser to accept the rise in average prices associated with relative price increases for major commodities such as food, which have low sensitivity to changes in aggregate income. For such products, large reductions in national income would have little effect on the volume consumed. Emphasis should be placed instead on trying to reverse (if appropriate) the basic cause of the relative price increases and on trying to prevent the spread of these price or wage increases to other sectors. Certainly, stabilization policy should not be highly stimulative at such times, and historical experience would suggest that a sudden or excessive shift toward restraint is extremely costly.

The third situation, that of inflation arising out of institutional factors such as a catch-up round of wage increases in an already slack economy, would seem to be one in which further demand restraint may be largely ineffective. In the labor market, wage increases are likely to be concentrated in the organized sectors, where the basic pressures are viewed as a response to previous price increases or as an attempt to match the previous wage gains of others in a continuing upward spiral, rather than as a response to demand factors. On the price side, cost pressures are intensified by falling labor productivity and increasing unit overhead costs.

The current inflation reflects a mixture of these factors. Between 1972 and 1974, external factors such as the food and energy crises were responsible for most of the acceleration of the rise in the consumer price index; but by late 1974, the inflation had spread to other sectors, and all components of the index were rising rapidly. During the recession that followed, the rate of inflation in consumer prices declined sharply, from 12.2 percent at the end of 1974 to 7.0 percent at the end of 1975 and to 4.5 percent for the first quarter of 1976 (at an annual rate). But this decline partly reflected near completion of the transition to higher energy prices and a better crop year, factors that were not directly related to the reduction in demand. Although the rate of overall wage increase slowed from 9.4 percent during 1974 to 7.9 percent in 1975, negotiated union wage rates advanced by about 10 percent in both 1974 and 1975. (In the first quarter of 1976, both series slowed down to annual rates of increase of 6.4 percent and 8.8 percent, respectively.)

A disappointing aspect of recent stabilization policy has been the inability of the combined efforts of fiscal and monetary policy to produce a more stable expansion of aggregate demand. Instead, they have sometimes operated at cross-purposes. There has been a sharp rise in the fluctuations of both monetary conditions and discretionary fiscal policy. This is true regardless of whether one believes that the appropriate measure of monetary conditions is interest rates or money supply growth. Monetary and fiscal policy actions in recent years seem to have been a net contributor to instability in the economy because they were often not taken in response to variations in private demand.

The increased instability of aggregate demand over the last decade is in marked contrast with the stable expansion of economic activity that was maintained between the trough of the recession of 1961 and the end of 1965, when we began to try fighting a war without a tax increase. Instability in aggregate demand is also, in part, an explanation of the sharp deterioration in the effectiveness of anti-inflation policy.

Lack of continuity in policy increases uncertainties about the future pattern of economic growth and greatly complicates the process of planning future capacity needs. More investment mistakes are made, a wider dispersion of capacity utilization rates among interrelated industries develops, and supply bottlenecks become increasingly severe. Thus, in an economy in which the generation of new capacity can take many years, sharp changes in the growth of real output, through their effects on profit expectations and on the cost and availability of capital (utilities are a notable case), can intensify the problem of capacity imbalances in the future. Indeed, frequent reductions in aggregate demand may relieve current inflation only at the cost of more inflation during subsequent periods of recovery.

This problem is well illustrated by the U.S. experience with supply shortages in several basic industries during the 1972–1973 period. The prices of such primary products normally rise during periods of rapid growth in world industrial demand. But the magnitude of the price increases far exceeded the increase in pure aggregate demand. In most sectors of the economy, measures of resource utilization were at modest levels, and the rise of demand was similar to that in earlier periods of more modest price increases. Instead, some of the specific capacity shortages can be traced to insufficient investment during the period from 1969 to 1971, when demand was depressed.*

We conclude that stabilization policy could be enhanced by a greater focus on maintaining a steady expansion of aggregate demand with respect to the growth of available capacity. If stabilization tools are used in this way, short-term emphasis should be placed on preventing excesses or deficiencies of aggregate demand arising in the private sector. However, we do not believe that the private sector is as unstable as the frequent reversals of fiscal and monetary policy have implied. Indeed, this variability has often been traceable to the shifting priorities of the policies themselves.

CHANGING RELATIONSHIPS
IN THE INTERNATIONAL ECONOMY

The impact on the U.S. economy of sharp increases in world commodity prices during the 1972–1974 period was a dramatic example of the extent to which the U.S. role in the world economy has changed. The disturbance in world commodity markets caused by such a sudden and steep price rise has heightened the public's awareness that international economic events can have major reverberations within the domestic economy. The reverse is also true; economic conditions within the United States continue to have a strong international influence, although they are no longer the major influence they once were. Clearly, economic isolationism is neither possible nor desirable as a response to these changes. Yet recognition of a different role for the United States in international economic affairs obviously requires an adjustment in the way domestic economic policy is conducted.

A liberal system of international trade and capital movements is of great value to the United States. If adequate supplies of some basic commodities were not available from other countries, the costs of complete reliance on domestic sources would be excessive. Increased benefits accrue to all countries when domestic goods with low comparative costs are exported and foreign products with low comparative costs are imported. The competition of foreign producers has been a major factor in restraining inflationary cost and price increases in domestic industries.**

*See memorandum by JOHN D. HARPER, page 87.
**See memorandum by R. HEATH LARRY, page 87.

In recent years, there have been major changes in the international financial system in response to the increasingly frequent crises in world capital markets. The postwar system of fixed exchange rates was replaced by a variety of adjustment mechanisms that involve greater emphasis on flexibility of exchange rates. There has also been a rapid expansion of international capital markets and of capital flows among countries.

The new system of more flexible exchange rates offers many compelling advantages over fixed parities. The necessary adjustment of rates to changing competitive conditions can be more gradual and can avoid the monetary disruptions generated by the periodic devaluation crises of the past and their accompanying speculative pressures. Flexible exchange rates also provide an automatic adjustment mechanism that prevents the transmission of excessive inflation in one country to other countries. Under the system of fixed parities, a rise in domestic prices would be reflected in a sharp decline in the trade balance. The increased export surplus of other countries, unless offset by restraint of their domestic demand, puts upward pressure on their prices. In contrast, with flexible rates, the domestic inflation of a country is partially reflected in a decline in its exchange rate rather than entirely in an export surplus for others.

However, there may be a need for some limited government participation in exchange markets to prevent the erratic short-run fluctuation that increases the risk and costs of trade. Nevertheless, such intervention should be minimized because difficulties arise in distinguishing between this type of stabilizing activity and the conscious attempts of governments to manipulate exchange rates for internal purposes. Sharp devaluations can also intensify the problems of a country in the midst of an inflation because they do not allow the breathing spell that can exist under a regime of more fixed rates. An artificially low exchange rate, for example, provides a means of achieving an export-led stimulus to the domestic economy by passing the burden of demand stimulus to others. Our 1973 policy statement *Strengthening the World Monetary System* examined the problems and issues of international monetary reform in some detail and is in line with the pragmatic approach taken by the Jamaica Accord. From the viewpoint of controlling inflation, it is important to emphasize that a liberal system of world trade and capital movements can make a valuable contribution to greater stability in world financial markets.

A single stabilization policy for all countries may not be feasible, but closer consultation concerning individual stabilization policies is desirable among industrial nations. **We recommend increased consultation and cooperation among industrial countries as a means of improving the coordination of their fiscal and monetary policies.**

World Commodity Markets

In an interrelated world economy, variations in economic activity within other countries will be of growing importance to the United States. Trade flows cannot be expected to respond immediately to changes in exchange rates. A sharp rise in world demand or a reduction in world supply would stimulate the demand for U.S. exports and drive up prices of imported commodities for which short-term substitutes are not available. This problem of potential instability of world markets is of particular importance to the United States because this country is heavily involved in primary commodity markets, where price fluctuations have been large and supply disruptions are most frequent. Some of these potential disturbances may be avoided by actions of the United States alone; others may require international cooperation. But although the problem can be reduced, inflationary disturbances in world markets cannot be completely eliminated, even with flexible exchange rates.

World agricultural markets raise special problems for the United States because of its extensive involvement as a supplier of over one-sixth of world agricultural trade. The U.S. share of world grain exports normally exceeds 50 percent. But world production of these products is highly variable and dependent upon the uncertainties of the weather. In the past, the United States has been prepared to be the supplier of last resort for the rest of the world; as a result, American exports have reflected most of the instability. The sharp rise in export demands since 1971, with its considerable impact on domestic food prices, has resulted in extensive public debate of this export policy. The rise in food prices and the response of domestic wages must be assigned an important role in any explanation of the current inflation problem.

But the major advantages to the United States of expansion of agricultural exports must not be overlooked. It is among the most efficient of the world producers, and the $22 billion agricultural export earnings in 1974 represented 23 percent of total U.S. exports.

The problem of agricultural exports lies with government agricultural policies, not with the exports themselves. When production and demand are extremely uncertain, the need for maintaining reserve stocks would seem obvious. It is difficult to see how the best interests of either consumers or producers can be served by alternating cycles of boom and bust.

We believe that government involvement in agriculture should be limited to smoothing out the year-to-year irregularities of supply and demand for major crops. The question of appropriate long-run prices should be left to normal market forces. The maintenance of adequate reserves would seem to be the best means of accomplishing this objective. In addition, the existence of adequate overall reserves (public and private) will reduce other countries' fears that the United States will not meet their needs in future years. This would substantially improve the long-run outlook for agricultural exports. For these reasons, our 1974 policy statement *A New U.S. Farm Policy for Changing World Food Needs* recommended a reserve stocks policy. That proposal merits repeating here. **We recommend that the federal government assume the principal responsibility for establishing stockpiles of key foodstuffs in the United States large enough to ensure an appropriate degree of stability of food prices, to encourage and take advantage of commercial trade opportunities when they arise, and to assume a fair share of the responsibility for meeting the emergency food needs of poor nations. Every reasonable incentive should be provided to encourage private stock building and to utilize the market system as an integral part of a stocks policy. The government should use incentives to encourage storage on farms, thereby keeping the national reserve in an optimum location for any eventual market.**

On the demand side, it is impossible to ignore the disruptive influences that sudden surges in food prices have on the domestic economy. As a major world supplier, the United States has an economic and humanitarian obligation not to resort to export controls unless they are governed by international agreement. The unilateral imposition of export controls only invites reciprocal actions by others or sudden attempts to diversify sources.

Certainly, any system of reserves will require the establishment of rules to prevent their use as a permanent means of affecting the level of prices, but the systems themselves are not difficult to devise. The cooperation and participation of other nations would be desirable, particularly in setting guidelines for using such reserve systems; but in view of the substantial U.S. role, such participation is not mandatory to initiating the program. It is also true that some problems can be anticipated. Because it is not easy to define the long-run trend of prices, some price fluctuation will remain; nevertheless, the extreme short-run fluctuations would be moderated. For example, the average level of stocks over several years might be required to equal a fixed ratio of average production; this would ensure that the trend of prices could not be permanently affected.

The ability of the United States to stabilize world markets for non-agricultural commodities by unilateral action is even more limited. Because the United States represents a small share of the market, the benefits of any stabilization measures such as reserves are broadly spread over the world market and the costs to the United States alone would be excessive.

The obvious repercussions of an embargo on crucial materials such as oil should provide strong strategic incentives for cooperative stock-piling ventures by consuming nations in order to obtain some protection against supply interruption. Yet, the limited progress made by the International Energy Agency of the Organization for Economic Cooperation and Development in carrying out the draft agreement on emergency oil storage is illustrative of the problems involved.

The 1972–1974 experience of sharp increases in the prices of primary materials in world markets has heightened concern about future shortages. Similar episodes have occurred in the past (most notably in 1950, following the outbreak of the Korean War) and have created fears of a chronic shortage of raw materials. But many of these fears were short-lived; the historical problem has revolved around attempts to reduce burdensome surpluses.

The impact of the international oil cartel, the Organization of Petroleum Exporting Countries, has led some observers to predict similar actions in other markets. But producer cartels are not really new, and the historical record suggests that they usually do not last; the development of substitutes and new competing producers force their collapse. OPEC is demonstrating a high degree of staying power, but the situation of oil is not typical of other primary product markets. Nevertheless, it is true that manipulation of the market, even for short periods of time, can have serious disruptive effects.

Export embargoes are often suggested as a means of alleviating domestic shortages or inflationary pressures. Recently, pressures were evident in the United States to take such measures for lumber, grains, and iron and steel scrap. Soybean exports were embargoed briefly. But such unilateral actions can have serious repercussions because the importing countries respond with interventions of their own to assure supplies.

The more realistic view is that problems are likely to result from temporary periods of scarcity traceable to insufficient investment in processing capacity. The typical pattern of long investment lags leading to periodic cycles of scarcity and surplus is likely to be increasingly severe in the future. As the list of industrialized countries expands, the potential for greater fluctuations in demand and problems of predicting future needs would seem to be increased. Clearly, both consumers and producers would gain from greater stability of demand and prices.

However, we believe that opportunities for immediate substantial progress in stabilizing world commodity markets are severely limited. We must be prepared for the possibility that further inflationary disruptions will occur in world markets. However, declines in the prices of many commodities during 1974 and 1975 demonstrate that market forces can still operate. Moreover, implications of instability in other commodities must be kept in perspective; the role of basic commodities other than food and fuel in total production is small. And we have scored one major advance in the food sector with the Russian grain agreement. The 1972–1973 period seems to have been extraordinary in that crop failures, the oil embargo, a restructuring of international exchange rates, and commodity shortages in other areas occurred simultaneously. In retrospect, it would appear that excessive speculation associated with this upheaval played a major role in some individual markets.

SECTORAL PROBLEMS

Some special inflation problems are raised by conditions in a few sectors in which the nature of the market structure limits the effectiveness of competitive forces as a restraint on price and cost increases. Major examples are the construction industry, medical care services, and public-sector employment. For these sectors, special measures may be required in addition to the general measures we have outlined.

Construction Industry

Internal structural problems peculiar to the construction industry have played a major role in the inflation of prices and wages. Although existing price indexes may include an inadequate correction for productivity improvements, it is evident that price increases in this industry have greatly exceeded those of the rest of the economy over the last decade. Rising construction costs have reflected increased materials costs, low labor productivity, rising land prices, and higher interest costs. In particular, sharp variations in monetary policy through their effect on construction and mortgage financing have led to cycles of boom and bust in residential construction and thus in the derived demand for lumber products and other building materials. Delays in resolving environmental issues have also prevented the development of a stable policy with regard to the harvest of timber from national forests. Adoption of the suggested measures for monetary policy, more careful lending practices by institutional lenders, and speedier decisions on regulatory issues (discussed later in this chapter) would help to eliminate many conditions in the construction industry that contribute to inflation.

But the industry's collective bargaining arrangements also contribute to the inflation. The process is characterized by a high degree of decentralization; agreements are not standardized among localities or among different crafts, and the craft agreements apply to different geographical areas. The industry, through a combination of unions, contractor groups, and political forces, has been marked by severely limited entry of skilled labor, particularly on the largest jobs. This local control is reinforced by factors such as the Davis-Bacon Act, which has been administered to require payment of union-scale wages on federal construction projects; the practice by which national contractors working in a local area agree to be bound by the local labor agreements and to schedule regular overtime; local building codes that restrict the development of alternative production techniques; and the lack of effective national machinery for resolving disputes.

In addition, the sharp growth of industrial construction has resulted in shortages of workers in the highly skilled specialty crafts, and pressures to complete a large project on schedule reduce resistance to wage increases. This latter factor is a particular problem of national contractors who have no ongoing concern with local labor conditions. By signing agreements to continue operations during a strike, with retroactive payment of negotiated wage increases, they undermine the bargaining position of local contractors. The large number of union agreements by locality and craft has led to frequent jurisdictional disputes and a haphazard wage structure in which wage increases for one craft become the springboard for the demands of other crafts in the same locality or of the same craft in nearby localities.*

The problems of frequent strikes and large wage increases became so severe in the late 1960s and in 1970 that the government reluctantly instituted a system of wage and price controls. In the 1971–1973 period,

*See memorandum by CHARLES KELLER, JR., page 88.

the Construction Industry Stabilization Board was successful in reducing both the size of wage settlements and the frequency of strikes. This board emphasized an active role for the national union and trade representatives in developing a machinery for settling disputes, and efforts were made to reduce inappropriate wage rate differentials among crafts and localities. The size of the average first-year wage settlement was reduced from 18 percent in 1970 to 5 percent in 1973. Unfortunately, the board and its program were terminated by Congress in 1974, and subsequent wage settlements increased sharply despite extremely high levels of industry unemployment. This initial rise probably reflected major catch-up pressures from the control period. Since mid-1974, the first-year construction settlements have dropped from 15 percent to 9 percent, but only in the presence of 20 percent unemployment.

Clearly, there is a need to increase the size of collective bargaining units in construction and to standardize wage agreements among localities and crafts. The current administration has recommended that a modified version of the Construction Industry Stabilization Board be reestablished. **We support the reestablishment of the Construction Industry Stabilization Board. We urge that through actions of either that board or the National Labor Relations Board the size of bargaining units in the construction industry be substantially enlarged.** Such a move would provide increased opportunities for eliminating restrictive work rules and practices and for improving productivity. *

In addition, greater efforts must be made to expand training programs for those highly specialized skills that have been in short supply, to further ease the entry of minority workers into construction unions, and to improve the mobility of existing workers. Competitive pressures could be strengthened by repeal of the Davis-Bacon Act, as recommended in CED's 1970 statement *Further Weapons against Inflation*. In particular, repeal would strengthen the competitive role of minority-operated construction firms. Until repeal occurs, administration that often stretches the law to require payment of the union scale should be improved. Major efforts should also be made to reduce cost overruns (including those from excessive overtime) and to reform and standardize building codes.

Medical Care Costs **

Rapid increases in medical care accentuated by the Medicare and Medicaid programs have both created major social problems and generated significant inflationary pressures. Overall medical care costs have

*See memorandum by CHARLES KELLER, JR., page 88.
**See memorandum by D. C. SEARLE, page 88.

risen far faster than consumer prices, but it is clear that much of the problem of price inflation is concentrated in the area of hospital service charges. Hospital service costs increased at an annual rate of 6 percent in the early 1960s, five times the rate of increase for all consumer goods, and at an annual rate of 14 percent from 1966 to 1970, the period following the introduction of Medicare and Medicaid.

No single factor can be identified that will completely account for the inflation of hospital costs. Accelerated increases in labor costs, wasteful capital expenditures, changing technology, and especially the inefficiencies and cost escalation encouraged by cost reimbursement, all contributed to rising costs. Hospital accounting practices and recent government regulations also contributed. However, the dominant factor seems to have been the sharp rise in demand induced by the rapid spread of insurance (public and private) and rising incomes. Direct patient payment of hospital costs as a percent of the total has declined from 63 percent in 1950 to 23 percent in 1974. Thus, while hospital costs per day increased by $109, from $16 in 1950 to $125 in 1974 (681 percent), average direct patient payments rose by only $18, from $10.50 to $28.50 (171 percent). The increased direct costs to the patient only slightly exceeded the rise in prices generally. It is not surprising that demand for more expensive medical care has increased rapidly when it can be financed by a slight rise in out-of-pocket costs.

Although improved efficiency can help to hold down medical cost increases, the major reforms will have to deal with the problems created by the inability of insured patients to seek and evaluate low-cost alternative means of obtaining health care and payment by cost reimbursement of fees for service. The decision with regard to alternatives to hospital admission is generally made by the doctor rather than the patient, and knowledge that insurance will cover the major portion of such costs creates an incentive to place the patient in the hospital, where treatment is more convenient but also more expensive. In its 1973 statement *Building a National Health-Care System*, this Committee recommended far-reaching measures that could reduce inflationary pressures in the health-care sector, including proposals for restructuring health-care delivery, for phasing and financing of national health insurance coverage, and for effective planning and use of resources. In particular, we recommended (1) **that financing be based on prepayment for an essential set of benefits, and (2) that to the maximum feasible extent providers of care be paid in accordance with fees and charges fixed in advance by agreement with providers and related to a budget that reflects efficient orga-**

nization and procedure. We believe that the application of the concept of the health-maintenance organization represents an admirable and efficient response to such a payment system.

Public-Sector Employment

Since the early 1960s, there has been a pronounced acceleration of some government wage increases relative to those in the private sector. In part, this may have reflected the need to attract additional workers into areas of rapid demand growth. But much of the change in wage behavior can be traced to the spread of collective bargaining to the public sector and an accompanying rise in the militancy of these workers. The rapid growth of public-employee strikes is viewed by some as a natural extension of rights that already existed in the private economy. Such a view reflects a belief that government is just another industry and that what works in one should work in another.

But in several important respects, the use of the strike threat in public-employee wage bargaining is not comparable to its use in the private sector. First, the curtailment of some public services can raise serious dangers to health and safety. Similar situations exist in the private sector, but they are more common at the municipal level. Second, the demand for these services is likely to be very unresponsive to cost increases because no good substitutes are available; municipalities compete with respect to the cost and quality of their services in only a very limited fashion. As a result, the strike is likely to be a very powerful weapon, and employees have little fear that wage increases will lead to loss of jobs.

Finally, public-sector bargaining is differentiated by major political aspects. The incentives on the employer's side of the bargaining table in government are quite different from management incentives in the private sector. The specter of the next election leads to a greater focus on the near-term implications of a strike or settlement. Public strikes greatly inconvenience voters, who may respond by voting out the current office-holders. (The incentives to settle are strengthened if the cost can be buried in the overall budget or deferred into the future.)

In addition, public employees within a municipality comprise a crucial special-interest group and voter bloc. To the extent that a community is a collection of special-interest groups with competing claims on the budget, the strike weapon gives public employees an important edge over their competitors. When used in conjunction with the vote, it can sharply affect budget allocations. Attitudes have changed with respect to the appropriateness of public-sector unions, but policies to cope with the consequences have yet to be generally adopted. The process of wage negotiation must be adapted to reflect the unique characteristics of the public sector, and if strikes are to be avoided, alternative equitable means of resolving disputes must be developed. A special CED sub-committee is studying this problem.

Comparability of Pay Systems. The federal government, in particular, has relied upon comparability formulas as a means of resolving pay disputes. In principle, we believe that this is a very promising method of settling some of the conflict over wage levels. Several difficulties have been revealed, however, in the process of defining the basic wage and salary structure. Many of the most common job categories in government are not found in the private sector. In addition, the wage survey, which provides the basis for comparison, tends to exclude lower-paid workers in the private service sector who compete directly with government employees. Nor is there any adjustment in the wage surveys for regional differences in pay scales in most of the job categories. Some private-sector jobs are seasonal; in such cases, annual income (which is not now used) is a more relevant basis for comparison than wage rates. The definition of comparability is also greatly complicated by major differences between the sectors in the value of fringe benefits (such as retirement pay, job security, and insurance).

The current federal pay system also contains too few incentives to improve performance; merit increases are infrequently used, and longevity of service dominates in the determination of annual increases. The problem of undue complexity, inequities, and lack of incentives is particularly evident in the military. Although the annual increases of wage and salary scales seem comparable to those of private firms, the average wage has also been increased by an upward creep of job classifications. Most of the problems seem to be associated with the determination of appropriate pay levels rather than the annual increments.

We recommend that the survey of private-sector wage rates used to determine wages of government employees be expanded to ensure a representative coverage. Because of the upward creep of job classifications, job descriptions should be periodically reevaluated. In addition, comparability should be based on wages and benefits rather than on wages alone. Such an improved survey may be useful to state and local governments that choose to adopt comparability systems as a means of resolving disputes.

Third-Party Arbitration. Any prolonged strike of municipal employees can have as disruptive an effect on a local community as far-larger strikes can have on the national economy because the services they provide are frequently critical to public health and safety. Thus, it might be appropriate in such cases to apply the procedures of the Taft-Hartley Act for critical industries in the private sector. These would include cooling-off periods, fact-finding, and the option of compulsory arbitration.

Reform of the Negotiation Process. Even within the present structure, some improvements could be made in the negotiation process. Consideration might be given to widening the jurisdiction of bargaining units to a state basis to prevent whipsawing effects on individual communities. The incidence of strikes might also be reduced by providing advisory assistance to communities with little experience in labor-management negotiations.

Significant restraint might also result if the costs of settlements were made much more explicit to local voters. The allocation of taxes among various functions could be specified in tax bills, and budgets should be structured so that the costs of pay increases can be clearly identified. Federal and state governments should ensure that the formulas for grants and revenue sharing do not amount to a subsidization of larger-than-average pay increases. Greater reliance upon user charges and tax districts that are coextensive with bargaining units are further means of clearly indicating to voters the costs of settlement.

Pension Benefits. Increases in pension benefits are a particular problem because the full costs are not apparent for several years and are dependent upon future trends in wage rates and living costs. Because of political emphasis on a quick settlement and low current budget costs, increases in benefits in public employment generally exceed those of the private sector. The costs could be made more apparent by converting government budgets to an accrual basis so that all costs of services rendered to taxpayers would be reported on a current basis, including current costs of pension benefits.

We believe that the trend toward collective bargaining in the public sector will continue, but the process will have to be adapted to meet the special nature of this sector. Laws prohibiting strikes are opposed by those who see an element of unfairness when strikes are allowed in the private sector, but efforts can be made to seek alternatives to strikes that would make it possible for critical services to be maintained. Also, when voters can be made more aware of costs, political pressures for a quick settlement are reduced.

GOVERNMENT OPERATIONS AND REGULATORY PRACTICES

Government regulation of business is justified by its proponents as a response to perceived cases of failure in the normal market system. Examples of such situations are pollution of the environment, inadequate industrial safety practices, potential health hazards, and industries such as public utilities, in which economies of scale make effective competition impossible or unduly wasteful of resources. However, the design of many of these regulatory processes contributes to the problem of inflation. The introduction of new regulatory measures can abruptly reduce available supply or increase demand. Existing regulations often restrict competition unduly and limit the market's normal adjustment mechanisms. In other cases, government regulations may favor a special-interest group.

For example, efforts to reduce environmental pollution enjoy widespread public support. The costs of controlling pollution should be reflected in the price of products. But sudden changes in pollution standards do not provide adequate time for adjustments in production and have resulted in the emergence of temporary shortages as a result of investment lags or curtailed production. Similar effects have been caused by unnecessary government attempts to specify the technology or means by which pollution is reduced. Many studies have recommended greater reliance upon incentive systems (such as charges or fees) that incorporate all costs to society in the price of a product and thereby keep all such costs low. For example, this Committee, in its 1974 policy statement *More Effective Programs for a Cleaner Environment*, supported greater reliance upon a system of effluent charges.

We believe that increased efforts should be devoted to measuring both the costs and the benefits of proposed regulations; alternative means of achieving the same objectives while minimizing the degree of interference with the normal operation of markets should be more fully explored. In addition, the alternative means of achieving a specific objective should be evaluated in terms of both their inflationary implications and their effect on markets.

Changing technology has made some existing regulatory measures obsolete. Control of railroad rates, for example, may have been justified when no competing modes of transportation existed. But this is certainly not the case today; alternatives are provided by airlines, buses, trucks, barges, and private automobiles. Indeed, a more serious problem today may be the setting of minimum rates for competing modes of transportation. Regulations that protect competing transport firms from competitive pricing and from entry of new competitors into the market may well deny shippers access to lower-cost modes of transportation.

Similar questions about the continued need for regulation exist in other areas of transportation, communications, and related industries. Numerous economic studies have demonstrated that present approaches to regulation are frequently ineffective in protecting the consumer against monopoly exploitation, that regulation has sometimes been introduced at the request of the regulated, or that regulation seriously distorts the incentives for minimizing the costs of production. It would be helpful to clarify the purpose and responsibility of individual regulatory agencies.

We support efforts to reexamine periodically the existing regulatory structure with a view toward revising or eliminating measures that contribute to inflation or unnecessarily interfere with normal market processes. Alternative means of achieving specific regulatory objectives should be evaluated in terms of their impact on inflation, on productivity improvement, and on the market system. In such a review, we believe that the burden of proof that regulations have been effective and are still required should be placed upon those who wish to continue them.

Even within the current regulatory structure, some of the rigidities could be reduced by speeding up the decision-making process and by allowing regulated firms to vary prices within specified ranges rather than requiring commission action on each adjustment. Some government regulation will continue to be necessary, but the methods by which this is pursued can be made more consistent with the efficient and flexible functioning of markets and with the objective of minimizing inflation pressures.*

The rapid proliferation of government licensing requirements and minimum standards requirements have also sharply inhibited the ability of the economy to respond to changing needs. In the area of public utility construction, for example, licensing requirements have drastically lengthened the time required to construct new power plants. Currently, it is not uncommon for a period of up to ten years to elapse between the initial planning and the start-up date of a nuclear power plant, much of it

*See memorandum by ROBERT R. NATHAN, page 89.

devoted to meeting multiple government regulatory requirements. Such long lead times drastically raise costs and increase the problems of accurately forecasting future needs. There are legitimate environmental, health, and safety issues involved in these actions, but it is crucial that decisions be made more promptly.

Finally, government regulations and licensing requirements have been poorly coordinated. Such activities are operated by a large number of different agencies that make little attempt to communicate or cooperate with each other. Too often, their objectives are in conflict with one another, and the burdens of delay and excessive administrative costs fall upon the private sector.

The inflation effects of government activities in other areas are closely related to the problems introduced by regulation. Too frequently, the timing of new program initiatives has reflected inadequate concern with the inflationary effects on individual industries. A familiar example is the expansion of financial assistance for the purchase of medical care for the disadvantaged and the elderly in the middle of the 1960s without prior efforts to expand or reform the delivery or the supply of such medical care services. A similar problem has resulted from large increases in grants for the construction of sewage treatment plants. On the tax side, both the structure and timing of changes in employment and excise taxes can have significant price effects.

We believe there is a need for a government effort to evaluate the price-stability implications of government expenditure programs, regulations, trade and agricultural policies, and tax measures. **We endorse the efforts of the President, through an executive order issued in 1974, to require "all major legislative proposals, regulations, and rules emanating from the executive branch of the government" to include an inflation-impact statement.** Primary responsibility for collecting, assessing, and publicizing these inflation-impact statements has been assigned to the Office of Management and Budget and to the Council on Wage and Price Stability.*

These new procedures are apparently proving quite useful in forcing government agencies to take more explicit account of possible inflationary implications of their actions and to explore alternative means of accomplishing their objectives with less impact on costs and prices. We believe, however, that more needs to be done to make sure the inflation-impact procedure is used effectively, including enlargement of the resources devoted to the program and extension of the reporting requirement to such regulatory agencies as the International Trade Commission.**

*See memorandum by W. D. EBERLE, page 89.
**See memorandum by HERMAN L. WEISS, page 90.

CAPACITY IMBALANCES
AND SECTOR BOTTLENECKS

Significant capacity shortages were experienced in several basic industries during the 1972–1973 period of economic expansion and were aggravated by the wage and price controls then in effect. These capacity problems developed despite indications, apparently exaggerated, that additional capacity was on average quite plentiful. As such, the period was illustrative of the dangers of exclusive reliance upon aggregative measures of economic conditions.

In a highly interrelated economic system, output can be significantly constrained by the capacity of small but important industries. Yet, the 1972–1973 experience must be viewed as highly unusual in terms of the number of disruptive events that had a simultaneous impact upon the world economy: the energy crisis, crop failures, and the importance of the U.S. devaluation.

In addition, the industrial countries experienced a particularly rapid recovery from the 1969–1970 recession, and this abruptly increased the demand for many basic commodities. Firms that had previously canceled expansion plans in response to the low production and falling profits of the recession were caught short by a worldwide rise in demand. Thus, the rate of rise of demand (rather than its level) created much of the problem because time was inadequate to adjust capacity. In some industries, such as paper, coal, and steel, changes in environmental standards reduced the amount of available capacity. In the case of wood products, an abrupt shift of monetary policy toward expansion directly contributed to the inflation by generating a 75 percent increase in home building within eighteen months. (Home building accounts for about one-half of total lumber consumption.) The shortages were amplified by the sudden injection of major government programs to stimulate low-income housing. Because of the rapidity of this demand increase, neither expansion of capacity nor the substitution of other products could be mobilized to moderate the effects on prices.

Clearly, no single factor was responsible for the rise in basic material prices, and much of the capacity problem has now dissipated as the result of market action. To the extent that such speculative binges are domestic in origin, they might be mitigated in the future by adopting the more general policy recommendations offered in this chapter. If the expansion of aggregate demand were less erratic, fewer errors would be made in forecasting capacity needs. Less reliance on monetary policy as a means of achieving demand restraint (made possible by a more timely and appropriate use of fiscal policy) would reduce the costs of capital formation and contribute to greater stability. Flexible exchange rates should make possible a more gradual adjustment to changing competitive conditions in world markets. The elimination of outdated regulations and speedier approval of licensing requests would shorten the construction period for new capacity.*

However, some additional measures might be considered. Recent events have clearly indicated the need for greater emphasis on micro-economic factors in the collection of data on availability of productive capacity. The highly specific capacity shortages that developed in 1972 and 1973 were not evident in the available aggregate indexes of capacity utilization. Furthermore, a lengthening of lags in the planning and construction of new capacity is inherent in the trend toward more capital-intensive production techniques in the basic commodity industries. Some consideration might be given, in a restructuring of tax laws, to creating greater incentives for firms to maintain a larger margin of stand-by capacity.**

*See memorandum by R. HEATH LARRY, page 90.
**See memorandum by ROBERT R. NATHAN, page 90.

Chapter 3

Curbing the Spread
of Inflation and
Stimulating Economic Growth

T he PROPOSALS OFFERED in Chapter 2 could make a significant contribution to the control of inflation by reducing the magnitude of the inflationary shocks to which the economy is subjected and by moderating the adjustment process. In reviewing the postwar history of inflation in the United States, we are struck by the importance of such disturbances, whether they originated in mistaken policies, international upheavals, or abrupt changes in domestic markets. But not all crises can be anticipated, and abrupt reallocation of resources will, on occasion, be required. Thus, we must expect that some unforeseen inflation-initiating shocks will continue to occur.

Beyond their direct impact on the price level, the problem with such shocks is that their price and wage effects cannot be contained within the specific sector affected. Thus, they are followed by a period in which cost increases induce price increases in other sectors and in which wages rise in an attempt to offset the higher cost of living or to restore parity with wage rates in other industries, occupations, or labor markets. Relative price changes are not achieved within a framework in which some prices and wages rise and others fall. Instead, virtually all prices and wages tend to rise, but at widely disparate rates. We have examined some of the factors that make this transmission aspect of the inflation problem so intractable.*

In the past, efforts to contain the transmission process have concentrated on restrictive monetary and fiscal policies to reduce real demands; subsequently, unemployment and idle capacity were expected to exert strong restraint on the average level of prices and wages. Admittedly, this process has not always been well managed. But in recent years, there has been a more fundamental difference. High levels of unemployment have not quickly dampened nor effectively stopped the rise of prices and wages, and inflation has occurred despite the absence of demand pressures in the aggregate. Thus, the primary problem is not that the available tools are inadequate to control demand but that restraint of demand does not necessarily imply sufficient restraint of inflation. Too much of the reduction in demand is absorbed initially by reducing supply, with only a gradual and long-drawn-out process of slowing the rise of prices and wages. Thus, although demand-management policies continue to be the critical element in any program for preventing the outbreak of inflation, demand restraint alone is not enough to stop an ongoing episode without involving excessive costs in terms of unemployment and inequities. The most recent recession has slowed inflation, but stopping it might well require unemployment in high double-digit figures.

Moreover, sharp reductions in demand during recessions disrupt the process of anticipating and constructing capacity, giving rise to greater future problems of shortages and capacity imbalances. Some prices fall sharply in recessions. But when they fall below the level required to earn an adequate return on capital, the result is reduction or cancellation of investment, future capacity shortages, and renewed inflation in subsequent years resulting from bottlenecks.**

In recessions, workers become concerned with job security and push for more restrictive work rules; the less well organized are closed off from the market for good jobs; pressures increase for political intervention on behalf of individual groups; and social tensions are intensified. For example, weekly earnings of nonagricultural workers, adjusted for inflation, declined by 7 percent between 1973 and 1975—below the level of income achieved as long ago as 1967. Some of this loss can be traced to higher food and energy costs, but much of it reflects large recession-induced declines in labor productivity and a shorter workweek. When real income declines are of this magnitude, they can trigger demands for compensatory wage increases.

*See memorandum by HERMAN L. WEISS, page 91.
**See memorandum by JOHN D. HARPER, page 91.

INDEXING TO ADJUST TO INFLATION

Because the problems of eliminating inflation appear so difficult to some observers, it has been suggested that the United States should learn to live with it, that economic institutions and contractual arrangements should be modified to reduce the most serious costs of inflation by a system of indexing, which would tie nominal values in contracts, laws, and regulations to an index of the general price level.

We believe that such formal indexing measures are more likely to intensify the problem by amplifying the inflationary effects of initiating shocks because they would be more immediately reflected in other prices and wages. (Thus, a system of general indexing would have intensified the 1972–1974 inflation, when external factors resulted in large price increases for food, fuel, and imported goods.) Nor is there any assurance that such indexing will moderate the demands of individuals and groups within the domestic economy for increases in their real incomes; conflict over the appropriateness of the existing wage and price structure would continue to generate inflation pressures.

But the major issue with regard to indexing is one of degree and balance among groups. The United States has already moved to protect the incomes of the poor and the elderly from inflation by including an indexing feature in social security, food, stamp payments, and retirement benefits for federal workers. In addition, other transfer programs are periodically adjusted by Congress to reflect price level increases.

The existence of cost-of-living escalators in some private wage and price contracts has intensified some of the distortions and inequities of inflation. When some contracts include cost-of-living escalators and others do not, unanticipated increases in prices distort the relative wage structure and create pressures for matching wage increases in other sectors. Wage rates seldom decline; therefore, an equilibrium wage structure can be restored only by further rounds of wage and price inflation.

However, there are actions that could be taken to reduce the inequities and the distortions of inflation without seriously increasing its self-perpetuating aspects. First, the current method of adjusting federal employee pensions for inflation raises payments by 4 percent for each 3 percent rise in living costs. **We recommend elimination of the excessive allowance for the rise in living costs that is now made for federal employee pensions. We also urge reconsideration of the excessive allowance for inflation that is now made for social security pensions.**

Second, because federal regulations restrict the rise in deposit interest rates at financial institutions, small savers who lack alternative investment options are penalized unduly by inflation. This problem provides an additional motivation for seeking reform of regulations in the financial sector. **We support a system of interest rate flexibility that would make possible the elimination of interest rate ceilings on thrift accounts and that would promote variable interest rate mortgages.***

Third, inflation (in combination with the present tax laws) seriously distorts incentives for business investment and intensifies the problems of financing required capital expansion. Although we recognize that changes in the tax structure involve complex issues of equity and efficiency, we believe that some changes will be required to ensure adequate investment incentives. CED, through its Subcommittee on Capital Needs, is currently examining this issue in the context of the nation's capital requirements over the next decade.

ADDITIONAL WEAPONS
FOR FIGHTING INFLATION

Although demand-management policies continue to be a critical element of any program for preventing the outbreak of inflation, demand restraint alone is not enough to stop an ongoing episode of inflation without excessive costs to the economy and society.**

In this chapter, we examine some of the proposed alternatives and supplements to demand restraint as a means of dealing with an upward spiral of wages and prices. These measures are grouped into two major categories: first, efforts that can be made to strengthen competition in some markets so that market forces could better succeed in dampening an inflation with a modest restraint of aggregate demand; second, proposals that involve a more direct government role in holding down inflationary wage and price increases.

It is our conclusion that no single proposal can eliminate the basic problem. The measures that could be taken to increase competition are in many cases the same as those proposed in Chapter 2 to strengthen resistance to the initiating economic shocks. But we recognize that there are limits to the extent to which the structural and social changes that we have enumerated can or should be reversed.

*See memorandum by R. STEWART RAUCH, JR., page 91.
**See memorandum by JOHN D. HARPER, page 91.

IMPROVING COMPETITION*

Several specific recommendations were made in Chapter 2 for improvements in competition. These proposals for improving the flexibility of the economy and speeding the transfer of resources in response to changing needs could make an equally important contribution to eliminating the problems created by the transmission of inflationary shocks. We will not repeat the recommendations here, but some major areas deserve special emphasis. First, for some of our most basic industries, freer international trade is an effective means of ensuring the maintenance of strong competitive pressures. Second, government regulations have frequently limited competition; delays in license approvals, excessive reporting requirements, and overlapping agency jurisdictions have sharply curtailed the ability of some industries to adjust to changing conditions. Third, as we have emphasized in earlier statements, a firm and clear antitrust policy remains the cornerstone of a competitive economy.**

In addition, improvements can be made in the functioning of U.S. labor markets. Although significant progress has been made in reducing barriers to employment based on race or sex, such discrimination continues to be a problem. Over the last decade, the United States has experimented with a wide range of manpower training programs. There is a need for a detailed evaluation of these efforts; a Subcommittee on Employment for the Young, Old, Disadvantaged, and Displaced is doing this.

Roles of Labor and Management

But any substantial progress in dampening an ongoing inflation is dependent upon improvements in the process of negotiating labor-management agreements. Except during periods of significant labor shortages, wage negotiations have seldom been a major initiating factor in previous inflations. However, wage settlements have played a major role in sustaining an inflation well after the initiating factors have been reversed.

An essential element of the collective bargaining process is the right to strike. But as the economy becomes more complex and interrelated, major or prolonged strikes can become extremely costly to wide segments of the public and to the economy as a whole. These potential costs can lead to a willingness to accept even the most unreasonable demands.

*See memorandum by JOHN R. COLEMAN, page 86.
**See memoranda by R. HEATH LARRY, page 91,
and by HERMAN L. WEISS, page 92.

In earlier statements, we supported efforts to supplement existing procedures of the Taft-Hartley Act and the Railway Labor Act. Current procedures have been ineffective in resolving labor disputes after the expiration of the initial cooling-off period. Congress has been asked to deal with such situations on an ad hoc basis, but political pressures to achieve a settlement can lead to neglect of criteria for a noninflationary agreement.

It would be preferable if private parties could develop their own alternatives to strikes as a means of resolving their disputes. Recent voluntary agreements by the steel industry and professional sports to submit their disputes to binding arbitration are examples of such measures. We do not believe that such alternatives can be legislated by Congress. But efforts can be made to encourage their adoption by private parties. In particular, government welfare and unemployment programs should not be used to subsidize strike activity.

INCOMES POLICIES

A wide variety of proposals has been suggested for more direct government involvement in wage and price decisions. Many of these wage-price policies have been used previously in the United States and other countries. Experience has varied greatly, but some general conclusions emerge. No single policy has ever worked for very long, and we do not believe that the existing proposals concerning incomes policies can provide a permanent solution.* Wage-price policies cannot be substituted for appropriate general demand-management policy because none of them has worked when demand was excessive. They inevitably create economic distortions. They can operate only with a high level of public support. Two widely discussed variants illustrate most of the major issues.**

Wage and Price Guideposts

The guidepost program of the first half of the 1960s was an attempt to formulate criteria for what represented noninflationary wage and price behavior at the level of individual firms and employee bargaining units. The general wage guide was that wage and benefit increases should equal the trend in *overall* productivity growth. If the average rise of wages was equal to that of productivity, unit labor costs would be constant and the overall price level should be unchanged. In addition, prices should decline in those industries where productivity growth exceeded

*See memorandum by JOHN D. HARPER, page 92.
**See memorandum by E. SHERMAN ADAMS, page 92.

the overall average but could increase where the opposite situation prevailed. Several exceptions were also made for industries where special shortages existed.

The guideposts provided a more precise basis for discussing publicly what constituted responsible wage and price behavior. In fact, their primary value, if any, may have been educational. In the aggregate, productivity growth is the basis of improvements in real incomes; and increases in money wages in excess of general productivity growth must result in higher average prices unless someone else accepts less. Price increases in excess of increases in unit labor costs have similar implications.

But in operation, the guideposts encountered serious problems. There were no incentives to induce individual bargaining units and firms to adhere to the standards. A general increase in wages in excess of productivity growth could only result in price increases without improvement in real income, but an individual employee unit would still benefit by pushing for the maximum achievable wage increase. The same was true for an individual firm in considering the implications of its own price increases.

The guideposts were dependent on jawboning and other public pressures to induce compliance. But this led to an inequitable focus on highly visible wage and price decisions. Such a discriminatory pattern of enforcement, if effective, increases the dangers that the guideposts will significantly distort the price and wage structure and lead to shortages and inefficiencies.

The application of the guideposts also frequently reflected a view that the existing structure of wages and prices was correct. The listing of exceptions was never an effective means for dealing with demands for change in the distribution of income. The use of guideposts tended to ignore the underlying conflicts over relative incomes that existed at the microeconomic level and referred to firms and workers as though they were monolithic units. In effect, the program did not adequately combine a general standard with criteria for an orderly resolution of conflicts over the relative wage structure.

Finally, the guideposts were designed to meet the needs and problems of the industrial and service sectors of the economy. Money wage increases equal to productivity growth were expected to result in stable consumer prices. But when consumer prices rise because of price increases for food and fuel or higher costs of government services, the average increase in real wages is less than productivity growth. Adding the rise of extraneous consumer prices to productivity growth should provide a wage guideline consistent with an increase in real wages equal to an increase in productivity, but this in turn would imply raising unit labor costs and would aggravate the rise in prices. This problem of how to allocate a loss of real income resulting from price increases from outside the industrial and service sectors was an important source of dissatisfaction with the guideposts in 1966, and the same problem contributed to abandonment of price and wage controls at the end of 1973.*

Wage and Price Controls

The adoption of a formal system of price and wage controls is a major step beyond guideposts because the attempt to enforce any set of wage and price standards inevitably involves the government in individual price and wage decisions. Although a system of controls is a response to the enforcement issue, the extensive government involvement brings with it many additional problems.

In the 1972 statement *High Employment without Inflation,* we supported the use of price and wage controls only as a temporary supplement to other programs of fiscal-monetary policy and structural reform.** We emphasized the need to move quickly and in an orderly fashion to supplant controls with policies that addressed themselves more directly to the basic problems. Yet, it is evident that controls became a substitute for, rather than a supplement to, these other policies. Little if any effort has been directed to implementing structural reforms of the type proposed in that report, and in retrospect, it is clear that the fiscal and monetary stimulus to demand in late 1972 was excessive. In addition, the original intent of the program was to restrain wage and price increases in industries where excess demand factors were not the driving force behind the inflation; but in subsequent years, events overtook the policy. By late 1973, shortages rather than cost pressures were the major contributing factors, and controls are not an effective response to such problems.** But the period also illustrated many of the fundamental difficulties that result from reliance upon controls as a long-run solution to the inflation problem.

First, controls can seriously impair incentives. The determination of appropriate prices required to balance supply and demand and provide adequate incentives for future expansion is a complex process; the complexity is particularly great for firms with high fixed costs and joint costs to be allocated among many products. Yet, small mistakes in determining ceiling prices can seriously distort investment incentives and lead to future

*See memorandum by ROBERT R. NATHAN, page 93.
** See memoranda by JOHN D. HARPER, page 94.

capacity imbalances. If prices are held below market-clearing levels, some scheme for allocating scarce products must be developed.

In labor markets, the process involves difficult political problems because major work stoppages can be avoided only by maintaining the support of the labor unions. Thus, under a system of controls, it seems inevitable that the resolution of conflicts over relative wages will become more of a political process and less reflective of economic considerations.

Second, any control system gives rise to increased pressure for more extensive government involvement in market decisions. Controls are initially viewed as a means of restraining wage and price increases in industries where competitive forces are insufficient, but the government is under great pressure to extend controls to other sectors where there is little evidence that their efforts can improve upon normal market forces. It is difficult for the public to distinguish between irresponsible price and wage increases and those that may be required to shift resources to areas of growing demand or to balance demand and supply of scarce resources. For example, the food industry is one of our most competitive sectors; yet, the public evaluation of the success of any controls program focuses upon grocery store prices. In recent years, the United States has had problems with rising food prices, but controls were not the appropriate response.

Finally, the United States cannot ignore the fact that it is part of a world economy. Attempts to hold prices below market-clearing levels will result in a shift to exports and a curtailment of imports. If rates of return are inadequate to attract capital, it, too, will move abroad.

In general, the complexity of the private market system and the distortion of incentives are strong arguments against any system of centralized price and wage controls. The experience of the United States and other countries indicates that these distortions and the political problems associated with them are fundamental difficulties; efforts to control prices and wages in peacetime have collapsed within a short period of time. They may be justified on a temporary basis during major emergencies such as war, but they do not provide a solution to inflation in normal times.*

Efforts to adopt wage and price guidelines or formal controls have also floundered on the problem of enforcement. Because of the complexity of the process of wage and price determination, government mandate and jawboning are poor substitutes for effective market forces. We believe that similar problems would arise with more recent proposals to use the tax system as an enforcement mechanism.

*See memorandum by CHARLES J. SCANLON, page 94.

EXPANDING SUPPLY
AND IMPROVING PRODUCTIVITY

A review of previous inflation episodes clearly indicates the importance of supply disruptions and low productivity growth as contributing factors. Yet, government policy measures in previous inflationary periods have emphasized restraint of demand while largely ignoring opportunities to expand supply. For the American society as a whole, improvements in productivity are the only source of sustained growth in living standards. Although output per manhour in the private economy expanded at an annual rate of 2.9 percent between 1947 and 1965 (3.5 percent during the 1960–1965 period of sustained price stability), it expanded at a rate of less than 1.1 percent between 1965 and 1975. With such a low growth of overall real income, it is not surprising that the conflict over relative incomes has intensified.

Over the longer term, we believe that greater attention to expanding productivity and to strengthening opportunities for individuals to raise their living standards through productive, well-paying jobs offer significant opportunities for moderating inflationary pressures.

To improve productivity and increase supply, it is imperative that economic policies be managed in ways that ensure adequate capital and effective investment incentives to meet the needs of modernizing and expanding the nation's stock of public and private capital, of improving the environment, and of stimulating new exploration for and conservation of critical materials. Short-run restrictions on private investment to reduce demand complicates the inflation problem in the future by lowering the potential supply.

As measures that would improve the incentives and reduce the risks of new capital investment, we have previously mentioned the importance of shifting the mix of fiscal and monetary policies, reducing lags in regulatory licensing approvals, and stabilizing the expansion of aggregate demand. In addition, the current structure of the tax system should be reformed to eliminate disincentives to investment that arise from the process of inflation. In particular, consideration should be given to adopting a definition of capital depreciation based on current rather than historical costs. Under present law, the effective tax rate on corporate profits rises with increased inflation and sharply reduces the availability of internal sources of funds for new investment.

Efforts to reduce the nation's unemployment problem through expansion of aggregate demand alone are likely to be highly inflationary. Thus, emphasis must be given on the supply side to improving the job skills of the unemployed, reducing barriers to the entry of minority groups into various occupations, improving the ability of unemployed people to move to areas where jobs are available as well as strengthening their incentives to seek out available job opportunities. Moreover, the current system of income maintenance programs (including unemployment insurance) should be reviewed and reformed to strengthen incentives and to remove disincentives to seek productive employment.

A policy of economic growth as a means of reducing the conflicts among competing groups to improve their standard of living must be premised broadly upon improving human welfare rather than strictly on more output of material goods. Economic growth should be consistent with the conservation of nonrenewable resources and reduction in pollution of our environment. But these are problems that result from the misdirection of economic growth rather than from growth itself. As we have argued earlier, the proper remedy is to improve the price system so that it more accurately reflects the true costs and benefits of various forms of economic activity.

TARGETS FOR REDUCING INFLATION

Any program for speeding the return to price stability in the aftermath of an inflationary episode must recognize that stability cannot be restored immediately and that measures directed to that end are likely to involve very serious social costs. Instead, efforts should be made to seek a gradual reduction of the inflation with recognition by all the participants of the need for moderating their wage and price demands.

We believe that coordinated efforts to achieve reduction of wage and price increases would be aided by the enunciation of goals and programs for lowering wage and price increases over a period of time. Such an agreed-on future program would provide a planning basis for private wage and price negotiations and serve to reduce expectations of future inflation. **A positive program for dampening inflation and restoring high employment should involve: (1) the adoption of a set of achievable goals for reducing wage and price increases over future years, (2) a coordinated mix of fiscal and monetary policies directed toward those goals, (3) supportive government efforts that are aimed at achieving** the voluntary cooperation of labor and business, and (4) a capital investment program to anticipate future shortages.

Organized labor and management, acting in concert, should play a vital role in such efforts. In the past, advisory committees of labor and management representatives have been an important source of outside advice to the executive branch. In September 1974, the President created a committee of eight business and eight labor leaders who would advise him on major economic policies and ways to assure effective collective bargaining, promote sound wage and price policies, improve productivity, and strengthen manpower policies. We believe that the President's Labor-Management Committee has provided an excellent framework for discussing problems of mutual concern and for providing the means by which labor and mangement can harmonize their differences.

We believe that the executive branch of the government should have the benefit of the discussions and judgments of a committee of high-level persons from management and labor. Although the committee's scope should include any matter of common interest, the committee could also provide a source of information and policy recommendations that could be included as part of an annual review of economic policy. The committee should be prepared to discuss and to offer opinions about achievable average rates of wage and price changes consistent with reducing inflation and unemployment.

Policy Coordination

We recommend that the President, in his annual economic message, propose a specific program with a projected timetable for reducing inflation, for maintaining a steady and sustainable growth of real output, and for returning the economy to high employment. The assurance of adequate jobs and rising living standards would reduce pressures for restrictive work rules and other measures that impede productivity growth. For wage earners, the continued growth of real incomes would have a moderating influence on demands for nominal wage increases. For businesses, the expansion of productivity through higher production and investment would provide an offset to cost increases as a motivation for price increases. A stable overall economic environment would also sharply reduce the problems of accurately anticipating future capacity requirements in individual industries. This is of particular importance for industries that have long lead times for the construction of new capacity.

We stress again that a more stable expansion of real output must be based primarily upon the improved coordination of fiscal and monetary policies. In recent years, these policies have frequently worked at cross-purposes, as Congress sought to stimulate employment with larger budget deficits while the monetary authorities attacked inflation with restrictive monetary policies. These divergent policies reflected, in part, different views about appropriate policy goals, and the way to harmonize these divergent policies remains a problem. Maintaining a policy mix of large budget deficits together with restrictive monetary policy will restrain capital formation and economic growth.

We believe that it would be highly desirable to shift this policy mix for any given overall level of demand stimulus in the direction of a somewhat easier monetary policy and less expansionary fiscal policies, thereby directing a larger share of private saving into private investment. This would be consistent with a long-term policy of attacking inflation by increasing supply rather than reducing demand. The recent reforms of the congressional budgeting process should increase the possibilities for such an improved coordination because Congress now operates within the confines of overall totals on expenditures and revenues. The new House and Senate Budget committees provide a forum for coordinating the fiscal objectives of the budget and the objectives of monetary policy in order to serve the goal of noninflationary economic growth.

We recommend that the current review of stabilization policy which is part of the process of setting the first and second concurrent resolutions on the budget be expanded to include a more explicit consideration of future goals for the economy as a whole and the appropriate mix of fiscal and monetary policies. This review process should require that both the administration and the appropriate congressional committees propose explicit goals for achievable future growth in real output and for reduction of inflation and unemployment and indicate their views concerning the appropriate mix of policies consistent with those objectives. Moreover, the Federal Reserve should be requested to indicate the general contour of monetary policy needed and the most likely costs and benefits associated with efforts to attain such objectives.*

We further recommend that Congress include as part of the process of determining budget totals a resolution indicating the consensus of Congress on appropriate goals for real output growth and reduction of inflation and unemployment over the next five years. Such a resolution would then provide guidance for appropriate fiscal and monetary policies in the future.

*See memoranda by JOHN D. HARPER, page 94, and by R. HEATH LARRY, page 95.

We also recommend that the recent budget reforms be extended to require a review and consideration of the budget on a multiyear basis. The practice of including in the annual budget document a five-year projection of existing expenditure programs and tax rates is a step in this direction, but similar multiyear projections of important proposed new initiatives should also be required.

Such a formal review process does not ensure that the goals for reductions in future inflation rates and for restoring healthy growth at high employment will be realized. But it does provide a forum for the discussion of differing views with respect to approximate economic targets and the implications of alternative policies. The intent of these recommendations is to promote the establishment of a coordinated national economic policy with greater continuity from year to year. In addition, the involvement of private-sector groups in the policy review should promote greater voluntary cooperation and provide some guidance for private wage and price decisions.

The government can undertake additional measures to encourage cooperation with the anti-inflation program. During periods of rapid cost increases without demand pressures, scheduled increases in taxes that add directly to costs (such as social security or excise taxes) could be postponed; and if demand conditions permit, some taxes might even be temporarily reduced. We do not believe that such tax measures should be tied to specific wage or price actions in a coercive fashion, but by being responsive to equity considerations, the government can maintain the support and cooperation of the affected groups in seeking to dampen the inflation rate. Temporarily lowering employment taxes would represent an effort to offset the effect of rising costs on prices. These devices can be used only on a temporary basis, but they may be effective in preventing a rapid spread and build-up of a wage-price spiral. In addition, during such periods of excessive cost pressure, the government should avoid the introduction of any major new programs that would intensify the upward pressure on prices or costs.

Finally, efforts can be made to provide better information and to focus public attention upon specific sectors that have encountered particularly difficult inflation problems. These activities are now a function of the Council on Wage and Price Stability. There may also be considerable scope, as we proposed earlier in this statement, for using a joint labor-management advisory group, in cooperation with the government, to explore more fully the range of opportunities for voluntary actions that would help break an inflation spiral.

THE INFLATION DILEMMA

Our analysis leads to a conclusion that many of the factors which complicate the adjustment to shocks and sustain an inflation process are inherent in the social and economic institutions of modern industrial economies. The analysis of inflation cannot be separated from other mechanisms that are highly social and political in nature.

We believe that the historical evidence clearly indicates that the adjustment to inflationary shocks involves a long period of gradual deceleration in the inflation rate. But it is equally true that reliance on demand restraint alone to speed the return to lower inflation rates results in excessive social and economic costs.

Opportunities for significant progress in the area of strengthening competitive processes, as a means of shortening this adjustment period, also seem limited from a practical point of view; many of the social and economic changes are not reversible. The alternative of greater reliance upon government-imposed controls has resulted in unacceptable distortions and inequities.

We conclude that there is no single policy that will solve the inflation problem. Instead, an appropriate policy will require a mixture of many different measures to supplement market forces. The new factor in inflation is primarily the increased magnitude and frequency of the shocks that disturbed the economy in recent years. The proposals offered in Chapter 2, if adopted, could significantly reduce the importance of these initiating factors. We have also suggested several additional measures that could be taken, within an atmosphere of cooperation rather than coercion, to reduce the degree of strife and the economic inequities that provide much of the continuing force behind the inflation process.

The Road Ahead

Some of the measures advocated in this report have been recommended in earlier CED statements but have not yet been implemented. Others are new, and we are under no illusion that they will be quickly or easily adopted. Nor are we confident that, even if our total program were adopted, it would successfully stem inflation and promote growth.

But we share four convictions. One is that a recurrence of the inflation experienced in the 1973–1975 period will bring with it very heavy burdens for many if not most of the people in this society. It is unthinkable that as a nation we would not take action to avoid such a situation.

A second is that the measures advocated here are worth trying and that all are within our capacity as a nation to implement if we wish to try them. Together, they give considerable hope that inflation born of new shocks and transmitted by new rigidities can be avoided.

The third is that the alternatives to trying such measures and making them work are most unattractive. Neither mandatory wage and price controls nor strong guidelines are consistent with a free, competitive economy; other approaches that we have examined also carry heavy costs for freedom and growth alike.

The fourth is that success in fighting inflation requires overcoming psychological barriers, specifically in countering the belief that inflation is inevitable.

Some of the measures we have proposed require strong action by government, by labor unions at all levels, and by private citizens. But many also call for leadership and action by business. The stakes are so high that only an all-out effort to adopt these measures and to make them work is acceptable. What is being tested is nothing less than the ability of a free people to govern their political and economic affairs in ways that would eliminate the excessive and unfair burdens of rampant inflation and high unemployment.

Memoranda of Comment,
Reservation, or Dissent

Page 11, by JERVIS J. BABB, *with which* FRAZAR B. WILDE *has asked to be associated*

When I read the first draft of this document, I was bothered by the omission of a Summary of Recommendations from the introductory chapter, a practice CED has long followed. I now understand why. A short list of exhortations to the federal government to do a better job, to cooperate more with other nations, to make further studies and reviews, and to have a policy about inflation is not a policy statement at all.

The paper discusses conditions, causes, and problems, but it provides little guidance to Washington on what the goals should be and how to reach them. Moreover, by generalizing about the factors that worked against a more rapid decline in the rate of inflation, it leaves a fuzzy picture of the magnitude and difficulty of the problem.

No mention was made of the amount total personal income increased in 1975 over 1974. No dollar value was placed on last year's decline in wages and salaries, caused by unemployment, shorter workweeks, and less overtime. Similarly, no estimates were given of the offsetting effects of built-in increases in wage contracts; increased pay and retirement benefits, based on the higher cost of living, to workers and retirees of private business and of governmental military and civil establishments and to those covered by social security; increased unemployment compensation; and tax refunds. Net of applicable income taxes, the latter group surely offset lower earned income from fewer man-hours of work by a substantial amount.

I oppose publication of this document as a CED policy statement, not for what it says, but for what it does not say. It is not up to CED's usual standard of excellence.

Page 11, by FLETCHER L. BYROM, *with which* CHARLES P. BOWEN, JR., E. B. FITZGERALD, JAMES Q. RIORDAN, J. W. VAN GORKOM, *and* FRAZAR B. WILDE *have asked to be associated*

The statement *Fighting Inflation and Promoting Growth*, as finally revised, adds little to the literature on the subject. Further, we make no new significant recommendations. I disapprove its publication.

Page 11, by EDWARD R. KANE, *with which* CHARLES P. BOWEN, JR., WALTER A. FALLON, *and* JOHN D. HARPER *have asked to be associated*

I must dissent from this study in two areas:

First, the report recommends that the management of fiscal and monetary policies be strengthened so that they can be used to fine tune the economy. I do not believe that fine tuning the economy can work. I would prefer that CED oppose the principle of fine tuning and not encourage the process by recommending changes believed to make it work better.

Second, in my opinion, government actions designed to reach specific output growth, inflation, and unemployment targets or goals, as recommended by the report, would be counterproductive and would yield less growth and more inflation. It would be preferable to correct the underlying structural problems of the economy rather than to attempt to force a predetermined level of performance.

Page 11, by FRAZAR B. WILDE, *with which* E. SHERMAN ADAMS *has asked to be associated*

Fighting Inflation and Promoting Growth is a well-written paper dealing with inflation, this country's major long-term problem. Controlling inflation is vital to our democracy's future.

The fiscal and monetary policies our paper emphasizes are basic in the fight against inflation, but will they be carried out with the consistency and emphasis they need? Considering the present political outlook, that is unlikely.

The public ignores basic economic verities and believes we will find ways to live with continuing federal deficits. Elected officials seem unable to withstand pressure from special-interest groups that enlarge deficits. Even leading economists are urging budget expansion, more tax reduction, and more monetary ease despite the fact that we are making steady economic recovery from a major breakdown. In fact, even the unemployment rate—the favorite economic issue in an election year—is improving nicely.

The question before us is whether this paper contributes to the control of inflation, which is already becoming a threat again. Present and upcoming labor settlements, with their open-ended escalation terms, are strong indications that inflation will return. In fact, basic price rises are here now.

Our paper recommends, primarily, that the thing to do is to adopt and maintain correct fiscal and monetary policies. Since this seems unlikely, it is important that we offer a backup plan. Some form of an incomes program with flexible guidelines for industry is the minimum that we ought to seek. Arthur Burns, our most knowledgable authority on cycles, has publicly suggested consideration for such a program.

The argument that any form of incomes policy has been proved a failure is not wholly true. We have never had any form of government intervention that failed to do some good, even though they have caused distortions.

We are told that inflation is on the decline. If so, the decline is inadequate. If we drop below a 5 percent compounded price increase in the next five years, it will be an unexpected miracle. Even that rate of inflation will destroy many of our cultural institutions. Our retired people will in a few years have to go on some form of welfare.

We are faced with a cost-push future.

One could go on with this horror tale, but why belabor the obvious. This paper needs a realistic second defense program. CED is not facing the real future by assuming this paper goes far enough in giving this country a workable formula for fighting its major problem, inflation.

Page 11, by THEODORE O. YNTEMA, *with which* E. SHERMAN ADAMS, C. WREDE PETERSMEYER, *and* ROBERT B. SEMPLE *have asked to be associated*

This policy statement identifies many of the aspects of inflation, but it does not discriminate satisfactorily among them. It is short on factual data and analysis of them.

Basically, the statement reflects the dilemma of conventional wisdom in trying to cope with inflation. The dilemma exists because most political economists and politicians are loath to recognize the role of labor organizations in amplifying and transmitting inflationary "shocks," or if they do recognize this phenomenon, they take cover in the view that appropriate institutional changes in labor markets are impossible.

The evidence indicates, in general, that during recent decades, the share of labor in national income rises in an inflationary surge and the share of profits declines (i.e., labor tends to amplify inflationary impulses, and business tends to absorb and dampen them). A chronic high level of unemployment accompanying inflation means that labor is overpriced if full employment is the objective. Moreover, the share of wages and salaries in national income, 75 to 80 percent, is so large and that of corporate profits after taxes so small, about a fifteenth as much, that persistent cost-push inflation is hardly possible unless fueled by the power of labor to raise wages even in periods of slack demand for its services.

Since the New Deal was launched in 1934, great institutional changes have occurred in labor markets, many of them designed to strengthen the bargaining power of unions and their control over wages. Despite some comments to the contrary, this policy statement really accepts the defeatist view that such changes are irreversible and cannot be substantially modified. In the short run, this may be true; and for the time being, we may have to resort to palliatives. Over the longer run, we can study and get a better understanding of the mechanics of cost-push inflation, and we can then devise means to lessen or remove the forces that produce it. Unfortunately, this policy statement contributes little to that end.

Page 12, by ROBERT R. NATHAN, *with which* E. SHERMAN ADAMS *has asked to be associated*

There is no basis for this observation that the problems in energy, food, and raw materials that combined to fuel the worst postwar inflation were compounded by allocation distortions attributable to wage and price controls. Contention that controls from August 1971 to April 1974 were a major cause of the 1973–1974 near runaway inflation is usually based on instinctive opposition to controls.

First, controls were effective only during Phases I and II. During Phase III, starting in January 1973, they were largely ineffective and were unevenly administered. Wages were more firmly controlled than were prices.

Second, most—but not all—of those in charge of controls did not believe in the whole control system. They could hardly contain their impatience for controls to end so they could express criticism of the system.

Third, across-the-board controls will, after a time and without flexibility, tend toward misallocation of resources, but price and wage controls in 1971–1972 cannot be blamed for the wild inflation of 1973–1974.

Fourth, the misallocation of resources resulting from the inflation and the recent recessions are far more pervasive and damaging than from the controls in the early 1970s. Inflation and recession severely hit housing, state and local governments, public utilities, plant and equipment outlays, and other sectors.

Finally, across-the-board rigid wage and price controls over time are undesirable and not needed. However, selective intervention and standby controls can be helpful. The chances of getting such measures have been greatly diminished by the poor administration of controls in the early 1970s and by the subsequent charges of total failure by many of those who had the responsibility for making the controls work to the best of their ability. We need such measures if we are to restore price stability.

Page 12, by JOHN D. HARPER, *with which* H. J. HEINZ, II, JAMES Q. RIORDAN, D. C. SEARLE, *and* ROBERT B. SEMPLE *have asked to be associated*

This paragraph gives no credit to the beneficial effects that have resulted from recent efforts to bring government spending under better control.

Page 14, by E. SHERMAN ADAMS, *with which* FRAZAR B. WILDE *has asked to be associated*

The report seems to imply that barring further inflationary shocks, inflation will obligingly go away and that while admittedly the "adjustment period" is hard to control, it is, after all, just a matter of making various adjustments, simply a passing phase that will happily come to an end.

I think this understates the seriousness of the process by which inflation is transmitted and magnified throughout the economy, commonly referred to as the *wage-price* (or *price-wage*) *spiral*. Unquestionably, one of the chief elements in the present inflation is the persistence with which wages and prices keep chasing each other upward. This process has proved not simply to be "very difficult" to control with traditional measures; it has proved to be highly unresponsive to them; and there is little or no evidence that they will yet succeed in bringing them under control. Nor is there much evidence that this spiral tends automatically to wind down. In fact, there is some evidence that it may tend to be self-perpetuating and even, in some instances, self-accelerating.

Page 14, by JOHN D. HARPER, *with which* H. J. HEINZ, II, JAMES Q. RIORDAN, D. C. SEARLE, *and* ROBERT B. SEMPLE *have asked to be associated*

I have been reluctant to approve this statement largely because it is built on the shaky premises that the inflation process has somehow changed and that its causes have become more complex. Throughout this statement, there is a tendency to view inflation as a short-run, fine-tuning problem rather than as an underlying, ongoing monetary phenomenon initiated by federal budget deficits and exacerbated by rising expectations on the part of business, labor, and the public that government spending will not be matched by revenues. Although the latest inflationary episode may appear to be different because of the oil embargo and the agricultural crop failures, these specific price disturbances were merely piled on top of an accumulative inflationary process that had been under constant growing pressure since 1960. Over the past fifteen years, the federal budget deficit aggregated approximately $150 billion, and the money supply, whether measured by M_1, M_2, or M_3, had increased from 100 to 260 percent. With two-thirds of the budget deficit and extraordinarily large increases in the money supply occurring during the latter third of this period, it should be no mystery to anyone why inflation worsened during 1974 and 1975. Furthermore, large government deficits and excessive increases in money and credit occurred in every country around the world that suffered from inflation. Too much effort and time are spent in this statement trying to explain how the latest inflation is somehow different just because some extraneous events occurred to complicate the demand-management process. Actually, the combination of excessive government spending and the printing of money to finance the deficit remains, as always, the fundamental cause of the inflation process. I think the tremendous improvement in the rate of inflation during the last twelve months is clear evidence that the conventional remedies do work and that the efforts toward restraint in government spending continue to be of tremendous benefit.

Page 15, by JOHN D. HARPER, *with which* H. J. HEINZ, II, JAMES Q. RIORDAN, D. C. SEARLE, *and* ROBERT B. SEMPLE *have asked to be associated*

This is a gross understatement. Over the past decade, fiscal and monetary policies have seldom been properly harmonized or applied in timely fashion.

Page 15, by JOHN D. HARPER, *with which* H. J. HEINZ, II, JAMES Q. RIORDAN, D. C. SEARLE, *and* ROBERT B. SEMPLE *have asked to be associated*

This is a subjective, unsupportable sentence. No one knows whether the conventional wisdom is enough simply because it has not been applied over any reasonable time frame. The evidence indicates that it does work.

Page 18, by ROBERT R. NATHAN, *with which* E. SHERMAN ADAMS *has asked to be associated*

Administered pricing and blunted competition must be acknowledged. No analyses of concentration and anticompetitive practices or the effectiveness of competition in the marketplace were probed in depth in this report.

A fifth structural change should be added to the four presented herein. It should deal with the behavioral and structural business changes leading to lack of responsiveness of prices in the marketplace to declines in demand for goods and services. We need to know much more about why prices have continued to rise at disturbing rates and why prospects point toward further distressing inflation, despite (1) three quarters of slower than normal growth in 1973, (2) five quarters of sharp decline in economic activities throughout 1974 and into early 1975, (3) continued high levels of unemployment and idle capacity through the middle of 1976, and (4) the prospects for modest and slow declines in the rate of unemployment for years to come.

Page 18, by HERMAN L. WEISS, *with which* E. SHERMAN ADAMS *and* JOHN D. HARPER *have asked to be associated*

Any listing of structural changes that tend to increase the inflationary bias of the economy should surely include the following:

A shift in the structure of our economy, in terms of share of total output and employment, *toward* those sectors with below-average rates of productivity improvement (finance, construction, services) and *away* from those sectors with above-average productivity growth (agriculture, mining, transportation, and so forth).

Structural changes in the work force, with increasing percentages of women, minorities, and youth, that make traditional programs to counter unemployment inherently more difficult to accomplish and more inflationary in their effects.

Chronic deficits in the federal budget that have increased the accumulated federal debt and induced an expansion of the money supply beyond that required to finance normal economic growth.

Page 18, by JOHN D. HARPER, *with which* H. J. HEINZ, II, C. WREDE PETERSMEYER, JAMES Q. RIORDAN, D. C. SEARLE, *and* ROBERT B. SEMPLE *have asked to be associated*

The most significant change has been increased government intervention in the domestic economic system in an effort to force the private sector to perform in some theoretical noninflationary manner while the public sector continues on its inflationary binge.

Page 20, by JOHN D. HARPER, *with which* C. WREDE PETERSMEYER, JAMES Q. RIORDAN, D. C. SEARLE, ROBERT B. SEMPLE, *and* HERMAN L. WEISS *have asked to be associated*

The implication in the latter part of this sentence is that the American economy is becoming less competitive, a concept that I reject completely. Labor's share of national income has trended upward steadily over the years and now constitutes more than three-fourths of the total pie; whereas the corporate profits share has steadily declined, especially during the past decade. Furthermore, manufacturing net profits account for only a nickel out of every sales dollar, and this is also smaller than in the mid-1960s. If big business has the power to dominate the American economy, as its critics allege, such power is not reflected in any profit figures.

Page 21, by JOHN D. HARPER, *with which* H. J. HEINZ, II, JAMES Q. RIORDAN, D. C. SEARLE, *and* ROBERT B. SEMPLE *have asked to be associated*

Contrary to the implications in the last two sentences of this paragraph, actual prices in the marketplace tend to be much more responsive to a fall in demand than the price indexes reflect. Whereas labor contracts often prevent reductions in wages when product demand slumps, actual transaction prices frequently decline even though product list prices do not. A large portion of the wholesale price index reflects merely list prices supplied by sellers, who have become increasingly unwilling to reduce book prices of their products when faced with the threat or prospects of controls imposed by a misguided Congress or by an administration that may panic from public pressure to do something dramatic when inflationary pressure grows as a result of excessive government spending. This paragraph implies that it is wrong to cut output when demand drops. I know of no basis for such a conclusion.

Page 22, by HERMAN L. WEISS, *with which* JOHN D. HARPER *has asked to be associated*

An accentuating factor in the 1973–1975 inflation was the decline in productivity. For instance, in 1974, when inflation was increasing at an annual rate of some 12 percent, productivity declined 2.5 percent; instead of mitigating price increases, it tended to accentuate them. The swing between this actual decrease of 2.5 percent and a "normal" increase of, say, 2.5 percent was 5 percentage points. This does *not* mean that loss of productivity was more important than, say, oil prices (estimated to have contributed about 3 percentage points to the 1974 inflation rate). It *does* indicate, however, that it was a substantial contributing factor, one that should be mentioned in this context.

Page 23, by HERMAN L. WEISS, *with which* JOHN D. HARPER *and* C. WREDE PETERSMEYER *have asked to be associated*

There is a persistent implication running through this section that size of firms and concentrated industries have reduced our economy's short-run responsiveness to changes in demand and increased the inflationary bias in the economy. Fundamentally, I believe that the market system adjusts more rapidly than any other or than is suggested here. And studies (e.g., by Professors Fred Weston of UCLA, Philip Cagan of Columbia, Yale Brozen of Chicago, and Steve Lustgarten of Baruch College) have shown that growth in size of firms (for whatever reason) is not, per se, a contributory factor to inflation.

Pages 25 and 66, by JOHN R. COLEMAN, *with which* ROBERT R. NATHAN *and* FRAZAR B. WILDE *have asked to be associated*

Our report is too soft at this point and on page 66. Competition—tough, impersonal, and relentless—continues to offer our single best hope that private economic decisions will work in the public interest. We rightly call for less government regulation in markets, and we attack certain labor-management abuses. But we fall back on less specific words in that area where government needs a bigger, rather than a smaller, stick: antitrust policy. Both documented stories and pending cases, even in a political climate not much attuned to militant antitrust policy, attest to the threats to free markets from some firms grown too large and too remote. Nineteen seventy-six is a good year to remind ourselves of the wisdom still to be found in Adam Smith's *Wealth of Nations.* CED should be aggressively and explicitly in favor of more old-fashioned competition than we now have.

Page 25, by JOHN D. HARPER, *with which* H. J. HEINZ, II, JAMES Q. RIORDAN, D. C. SEARLE, ROBERT B. SEMPLE, *and* HERMAN L. WEISS *have asked to be associated*

This sentence is pure conjecture, with little or no empirical evidence to support the implication that there is less competition in more concentrated industries.

Page 25, by R. HEATH LARRY, *with which* JOHN D. HARPER *has asked to be associated*

Price competition does not depend on the existence of a large number of firms, nor can the number of firms in an industry be used as a proxy for the degree of price competition.

Page 28, by R. HEATH LARRY

This sentence, in the context of the one that follows it, seems to connote that distribution of income (and the related matters of wages and prices) should be based on political rather than economic considerations. Such an approach is inconsistent with the general thrust of the overall CED statement, and exception must be taken to it.

Page 42, by THEODORE O. YNTEMA *with which* ROBERT B. SEMPLE has *asked to be associated*

The discussion of fiscal versus monetary policy does not take into account adequately the "crowding out" caused by selling an enormous federal deficit to savers. This process mops up huge amounts of private savings that otherwise would go into the financial markets, resulting in lower long-term interest rates and higher equity prices. The consequences of restricting capacity in industry and housing should not be underestimated.

Page 42, by JOHN D. HARPER, *with which* H. J. HEINZ, II, C. WREDE PETERSMEYER, JAMES Q. RIORDAN, D. C. SEARLE, *and* ROBERT B. SEMPLE *have asked to be associated*

There is no recorded instance in all of history in any country in the world where inflation was not caused by excessive increases in money supply relative to output. Whenever government spending exceeds revenue, it must finance the resulting deficit by running the printing presses. This causes a rise in the general price level, which is inflation. The following different causes cited merely reflect symptoms of the real cause.

Page 45, by JOHN D. HARPER, *with which* H. J. HEINZ, II, JAMES Q. RIORDAN, D. C. SEARLE, *and* ROBERT B. SEMPLE *have asked to be associated*

This ignores the effect of wage and price controls.

Page 45, by R. HEATH LARRY

There is no proof of this statement. In certain domestic industries, imports and the continuing prospects of large and growing imports have severely restrained modernization, expansion, and job creation. Because of inadequate domestic capacity, severe shortages have developed in the not-too-distant past, with import prices quickly rising to substantial premiums over domestic prices. The impact of past imports will continue to be felt in the future through insufficient domestic capacity.

Page 51, by CHARLES KELLER, JR.

It should be pointed out that the pressure to complete these large projects on schedule is exerted by the owners on the contractors. These owners are usually the major industrial and utility corporations and are also usually responsible for requiring their national contractors to continue construction during local strikes and to schedule regular, sometimes excessive overtime. The Construction Round Table has been successful in moderating these undesirable practices.

Page 52, by CHARLES KELLER, JR.

After over twenty-five years as the chief executive of a construction company, and one who was involved in labor negotiations at the local and national level, and as a strong believer in free enterprise and the desirability of avoiding to the greatest extent possible government interference in private business, it is with the greatest reluctance that I support the reestablishment of the Construction Industry Stabilization Board or some similar entity established and empowered by federal legislation. I am fully convinced that due to the factors outlined in this discussion of the construction industry, the industry is unable to discipline itself without the use of federal sanctions.

Page 52, by D. C. SEARLE

The Committee does itself little service by referring to its 1973 statement *Building a National Health-Care System.* That publication was not primarily focused on reducing the cost of effective health care and endorsed a number of proposals, including the use of price and wage controls, which the Committee now rejects.

Furthermore, recent experience has shown that there may be a one-time reduction in the cost of medical care for some people who switch from purchasing health care on a fee-for-service basis to the Health Maintenance Organization concept. However, after that one-shot saving, the rate of cost inflation for the two types of services run about the same. In my opinion, a great deal more work needs to be done before CED concludes that the problem of spiraling health-care costs can be effectively dealt with by the recommendations contained in the 1973 statement *Building a National Health-Care System.*

Page 58, by ROBERT R. NATHAN

Periodic review of regulations and regulatory processes and evaluation of the inflationary impacts of new regulatory activities are desirable.

However, more inflation may be associated with deregulation. Substituting competition for regulation might well result in a much higher degree of concentration than now prevails. Total or even partial deregulation may not achieve more competition. Greater concentration could well bring the opposite results.

We ought to favor more scrutiny, more frequent evaluations and improvements in the regulatory process, but we ought to proceed very cautiously in terminating existing regulation. Deregulation of the airline industry may leave us with only three or four major airlines and severe curtailment, if not elimination, of services that can have significant adverse cost impacts on many functions and in many locations.

Page 59, by W. D. EBERLE, *with which* E. SHERMAN ADAMS, JOSEPH L. BLOCK, JOHN D. HARPER, H. J. HEINZ, II, *and* HERMAN L. WEISS *have asked to be associated*

The requirement for inflation-impact statements by presidential executive order, although desirable in principle, is not adequate.

First, the order expires on December 31, 1976. Second, the order by its terms, only applies to "Executive branch agencies" and is not binding on the independent regulatory agencies. Third, recent court cases have raised serious doubt whether the President has authority to require an agency to consider criteria that are not set forth in the agency's statutory charter. Fourth, the actual implementation of the inflation impact has been marked by stalling and/or an inadequate response that defeat the real purpose of the order.

What is needed is an economic-impact statement to be required by an act of Congress and to consist of an assessment of the anticipated benefits of the proposed regulation, the costs of the regulation, their impact on various sectors of the economy, and an analysis of costs and benefits of alternatives to the proposed regulation. The Office of Management and Budget should be required to issue technical guidelines for the preparation of economic-impact statements as applicable to the differing objectives at various agencies.

This finding would be subject to public comment in the rule-making process and the basis for agency action. Informing Congress and the public in advance of the economic impact of any proposed action would serve to provide wider understanding of the need or lack of need for any regulation subsequently adopted.

The result should be that agencies, under law, would be on the open, public record as to their economic assessment in a specific, pragmatic way. This should make agencies more thoughtful and minimize needless economic burdens or expose excessive mistakes to the public for correction. Public reporting should create responsible accountability.

Page 59, by HERMAN L. WEISS, *with which* JOHN D. HARPER *has asked to be associated*

Congress, too, should follow through on the requirement, already existing in the House but essentially neglected, to prepare and evaluate inflation-impact statements in conjunction with significant legislative proposals of its own.

Page 61, by R. HEATH LARRY, *with which* JOHN D. HARPER *has asked to be associated*

The "capacity problem" has not been solved in many basic American industries; it has only been obscured by the recent recession. Before the recovery continues too much longer, shortages of certain materials will again become apparent.

Page 61, by ROBERT R. NATHAN

Modernization and expansion of productive facilities are essential if our economy is to expand and adequate job opportunities are to be available. Policies should be designed to encourage margins of some excess capacity and the rapid replacement of obsolete facilities. The distortions and misallocations of resources associated with inflation and recession serve to impede progress in this respect.

Plant and equipment outlays tend to drop sharply in times of recession. Then, during recovery, bottlenecks tend to emerge and cannot be quickly overcome. If we could avoid or shorten recessions, we would have higher aggregate levels of investment and less likelihood of inadequate capacity and bottlenecks in periods of full employment.

Policy makers are now talking about another recession if inflation persists or gets worse. They should be reminded that some of the reasons for threats of further inflation can be traced to the very low level of plant and equipment investments in this recession. Thus, resort to recessions as the major means of fighting inflation tends to be counterproductive.

Page 63, by HERMAN L. WEISS

A particularly aggravating factor is the "pass-on" problem. Although most of the direct effects of increased food and energy prices have already been passed on through the price structure, inflation still continues, in part because individuals and groups try to adjust by passing on their losses of real income to others.

Page 63, by JOHN D. HARPER, *with which* H. J. HEINZ, II, JAMES Q. RIORDAN, D. C. SEARLE, *and* ROBERT B. SEMPLE *have asked to be associated*

Bottlenecks that lead to higher prices of certain products may lead to changes in relative prices, but they cannot cause renewed inflation. This can only happen when the general price level rises in response to a disproportionate increase in the money supply relative to total output.

Page 65, by R. STEWART RAUCH, JR.

The ability to make variable interest rate mortgage loans is a desirable but not a sufficient prerequisite for the removal of ceilings on thrift deposit interest rates. To make such interest rate flexibility practical and realistic, congressional concern for housing must be satisfied by effective, noninflationary alternatives to the present system of housing finance, of which interest rate ceilings are a part. Moreover, flexibility also requires extensive structural reform of depository institutions, such as that proposed in the Financial Institutions Act of 1975, and adequate time for adjustment.

Page 65, by JOHN D. HARPER, *with which* H. J. HEINZ, II, JAMES Q. RIORDAN, D. C. SEARLE, *and* ROBERT B. SEMPLE *have asked to be associated*

Demand-management policies are not just a critical element for preventing the outbreak of inflation, they are *the* principal element.

Page 66, by R. HEATH LARRY

Rather than ensuring "strong competitive pressures," additional imports may effectively eliminate actual or prospective domestic competition (because of inadequate profit prospects).

Page 66, by HERMAN L. WEISS, *with which* JOHN D. HARPER *has asked to be associated*

If the implication is that strong antitrust action is needed against price-fixing and market allocation I, of course, concur. If, however, the suggestion is that antitrust action is needed against concentrated industries and size per se, I disagree (see my note on page 23).

Page 67, by JOHN D. HARPER, *with which* H. J. HEINZ, II, JAMES Q. RIORDAN, D. C. SEARLE, *and* ROBERT B. SEMPLE *have asked to be associated*

I doubt that they can provide any solution, even temporary, since individual wage and price decisions are only symptomatic of basic inflation caused by excessive government spending that is accommodated by excessive money creation.

Page 67, by E. SHERMAN ADAMS, *with which* ROBERT R. NATHAN *and* FRAZAR B. WILDE *have asked to be associated*

This section on incomes policies seems to me unsatisfactory. It starts with a rapid-fire recital of objections to this general approach, but it should be noted that almost all these objections would apply to almost any conceivable proposal that might effectively help to combat cost-push inflation. It then discusses and condemns two specific variants, guideposts and wage-price controls, implying that there are no other alternatives even worth talking about.

I beg to differ. It is a striking fact that the United States has never even *tried* a carefully conceived incomes policy. We have long assumed—or at least hoped—that the collective bargaining process as it happens to be presently constituted would somehow produce results that would be in the public interest. But we *know* that it is not working that way today, and the prospects that it will do so in the future are far from bright. Labor and management are the sole participants in this momentous process, and although both of these participants seem to be doing reasonably well, the public definitely is not.

I submit that the public interest deserves more weight than it is presently accorded in the determination of prices and wages. The public has a right to protect itself against unreasonable actions by labor or management that vitally affect its welfare.

Is it objected that prices and wages should be determined by "market forces"? Well, the public *is* the market, and the citizenry has a perfectly legitimate claim for status as a "market force."

There are of course various alternative measures that might be tried. One was proposed a few months ago by Federal Reserve Chairman Arthur F. Burns: "A policy which would permit modest delay of key wage and price increases, thus providing opportunity for quiet government intervention and the mobilization of public opinion, may yet be of significant benefit in reducing abuse of private economic power."

Naturally, several objections can be raised to this particular proposal, but please remember that this is true of any proposal for effective action. If we are really serious about trying to deal with the present inflationary trend in our economy and prevent it from becoming chronic and possibly disastrous, we should not be easily deterred from considering approaches that are not unreasonable and that might help us to cope with this enormously important problem.

Page 69, by ROBERT R. NATHAN, *with which* E. SHERMAN ADAMS *has asked to be associated*

Wage and price guideposts may not offer an ideal solution to restore price stability and they do pose problems, but inflation poses worse problems.

This report focuses on the dangers and harm of inflation. It is recognized that inflation's cancerlike consequences cannot be tolerated. But when it comes to suggested solutions like guideposts, all the difficulties and limitations are highlighted, whereas potential positive benefits are minimized.

We can structure guideposts and guidelines, and we can establish selective interventions in cost and price determinations that will minimize the adverse effects and maximize the positive prospects of bringing an end to inflation. Total success will be elusive, but if we truly believe that inflation is dangerous and harmful and costly, then we ought to be far more willing to resort to a variety of the measures mentioned but not supported in this report.

Similarly, the functioning of the marketplace can be much improved if we are willing to regard monopolistic and administered-pricing practices as truly damaging and subject such practices to harsh penalties. Corrective measures must be far more daring than set forth in this report.

A cure can be even more damaging than the disease, and we need to exercise care as well as courage in pursuing cures. A specific measure we might well undertake is a thoroughgoing investigation of competition and market forces similar to that achieved by the Temporary National Economic Committee in the 1930s. The more we know about the free enterprise and marketplace economy, the better able we will be to correct its weaknesses and enhance its strengths.

Page 69, by JOHN D. HARPER, *with which* H. J. HEINZ, II, JAMES Q. RIORDAN, D. C. SEARLE, *and* ROBERT B. SEMPLE *have asked to be associated*

I was one of the trustees who rejected the use of mandatory controls in 1972, just as I had rejected the use of voluntary controls in the 1970 statement. The inability of either type of controls to halt inflation is due to the fact that prices and wages in the private sector are merely symptoms of the underlying inflationary forces emanating from the mismanagement of monetary and fiscal policies on the part of government officials and representatives.

Page 69, by JOHN D. HARPER, *with which* H. J. HEINZ, II, JAMES Q. RIORDAN, D. C. SEARLE, *and* ROBERT B. SEMPLE *have asked to be associated*

In fact, controls often cause shortages because exports are stimulated when domestic prices are held below world prices.

Page 70, by CHARLES J. SCANLON, *with which* CHARLES P. BOWEN, JR., JOHN D. HARPER, *and* C. WREDE PETERSMEYER *have asked to be associated*

I would have preferred a forthright statement that the recent and past history of wage and price controls in the United States and abroad has been one of failure. I am convinced that such controls have not only failed in achieving their objectives but, in fact, have probably been counterproductive.

Recognizing the position taken by CED in the 1972 statement *High Employment without Inflation*, I would still favor this paper containing a strong unequivocal *recommendation* against the use of wage and price controls.

Page 74, by JOHN D. HARPER, *with which* H. J. HEINZ, II, JAMES Q. RIORDAN, D. C. SEARLE, ROBERT B. SEMPLE, *and* HERMAN L. WEISS *have asked to be associated*

Admittedly, policies and actions among the various government agencies should be better coordinated and integrated. However, this paragraph sounds like a pitch for national planning, which I strongly oppose.

Page 74, by R. HEATH LARRY, *with which* CHARLES P. BOWEN, JR., JOHN D. HARPER, *and* C. WREDE PETERSMEYER *have asked to be associated*

Establishment of specific national economic goals or targets would sooner or later involve establishment of economic controls to see that the goals or targets are achieved. Whenever such goals are not achieved, substantial pressures will inevitably develop for more government involvement. "National economic planning" has led many other nations into highly undesirable situations from which they cannot recover. It should be totally rejected.

Objectives of the Committee for Economic Development

For three decades, the Committee for Economic Development has had a respected influence on business and public policy. Composed of two hundred leading business executives and educators, CED is devoted to these two objectives:

To develop, through objective research and informed discussion, findings and recommendations for private and public policy which will contribute to preserving and strengthening our free society, achieving steady economic growth at high employment and reasonably stable prices, increasing productivity and living standards, providing greater and more equal opportunity for every citizen, and improving the quality of life for all.

To bring about increasing understanding by present and future leaders in business, government, and education and among concerned citizens of the importance of these objectives and the ways in which they can be achieved.

CED's work is supported strictly by private voluntary contributions from business and industry, foundations, and individuals. It is independent, nonprofit, nonpartisan, and nonpolitical.

The two hundred trustees, who generally are presidents or board chairmen of corporations and presidents of universities, are chosen for their individual capacities rather than as representatives of any particular interests. By working with scholars, they unite business judgment and experience with scholarship in analyzing the issues and developing recommendations to resolve the economic problems that constantly arise in a dynamic and democratic society.

Through this business-academic partnership, CED endeavors to develop policy statements and other research materials that commend themselves as guides to public and business policy; for use as texts in college economics and political science courses and in management training courses; for consideration and discussion by newspaper and magazine editors, columnists, and commentators; and for distribution abroad to promote better understanding of the American economic system.

CED believes that by enabling businessmen to demonstrate constructively their concern for the general welfare, it is helping business to earn and maintain the national and community respect essential to the successful functioning of the free enterprise capitalist system.

89447

Honorary Trustees

Statements on National Policy
Issued by the Research
and Policy Committee
(publications in print)

Fighting Inflation and Promoting Growth *(August 1976)*

Improving Productivity in State and Local Government *(March 1976)*

*International Economic Consequences of High-Priced Energy *(September 1975)*

Broadcasting and Cable Television:
  Policies for Diversity and Change *(April 1975)*

Achieving Energy Independence *(December 1974)*

A New U.S. Farm Policy for Changing World Food Needs *(October 1974)*

Congressional Decision Making for National Security *(September 1974)*

*Toward a New International Economic System:
  A Joint Japanese-American View *(June 1974)*

More Effective Programs for a Cleaner Environment *(April 1974)*

The Management and Financing of Colleges *(October 1973)*

Strengthening the World Monetary System *(July 1973)*

Financing the Nation's Housing Needs *(April 1973)*

Building a National Health-Care System *(April 1973)*

*A New Trade Policy Toward Communist Countries *(September 1972)*

High Employment Without Inflation:
  A Positive Program for Economic Stabilization *(July 1972)*

Reducing Crime and Assuring Justice *(June 1972)*

Military Manpower and National Security *(February 1972)*

The United States and the European Community *(November 1971)*

Statements issued in association with CED counterpart organizations in foreign countries.

Improving Federal Program Performance *(September 1971)*

Social Responsibilities of Business Corporations *(June 1971)*

Education for the Urban Disadvantaged:
  From Preschool to Employment *(March 1971)*

Further Weapons Against Inflation *(November 1970)*

Making Congress More Effective *(September 1970)*

*Development Assistance to Southeast Asia *(July 1970)*

Training and Jobs for the Urban Poor *(July 1970)*

Improving the Public Welfare System *(April 1970)*

Reshaping Government in Metropolitan Areas *(February 1970)*

Economic Growth in the United States *(October 1969)*

Assisting Development in Low-Income Countries *(September 1969)*

*Nontariff Distortions of Trade *(September 1969)*

Fiscal and Monetary Policies for Steady Economic Growth *(January 1969)*

Financing a Better Election System *(December 1968)*

Innovation in Education: New Directions for the American School *(July 1968)*

Modernizing State Government *(July 1967)*

*Trade Policy Toward Low-Income Countries *(June 1967)*

How Low Income Countries Can Advance Their Own Growth *(September 1966)*

Modernizing Local Government *(July 1966)*

A Better Balance in Federal Taxes on Business *(April 1966)*

Budgeting for National Objectives *(January 1966)*

Educating Tomorrow's Managers *(October 1964)*

Improving Executive Management in the Federal Government *(July 1964)*

Trade Negotiations for a Better Free World Economy *(May 1964)*

Economic Literacy for Americans *(March 1962)*

Statements issued in association with CED counterpart organizations in foreign countries.